The Red Prussians: East German and Soviet Plans for Conquest of West Germany During the Cold War
By Nevin Gussack

The Soviets always sought to bring Germany into its revolutionary fold. Germany was long the home of heavy and high tech industries, a vast proletariat, and served as a geographical gateway to Western Europe. Hence, a possible conquest of Germany represented a crown in the jewel of world communism. Since the 1870s and 1880s, Bismarck, the Social Democrats, elements of the Nazi Party, and elements in West German society all supported an entente with Moscow against the West. Bearing these factors in mind, Lenin predicted that *"Whoever has Germany has Europe."*[1] After World War II, the Soviets and their East German satraps all desired the conquest of West Germany for its technological innovations, industrial base, and for the increase in communist-held territory. West Germany also shared borders with France, Austria, Denmark, the Low Countries, and Switzerland. This geographical advantage would have allowed communist forces a strategic springboard to roll their tanks and troops further into the heart of Western Europe, thus destroying the NATO alliance. Soviet undercover KGB officer Ilya Dzhirkvelov highlighted the strategic importance of West Germany in a conversation with Khrushchev's son in law Alexei Adzhubei: *"With West Germany in our hands we would control the whole of Western Europe and could liquidate NATO, because West Germany is NATO's striking force."*[2]

Despite protestations to the contrary, the Soviets desired the reunification of Germany either as a neutralist, socialist state or under an outright communist occupation by the forces of Moscow and East Berlin. Stalin met with the leaders of the German Communist Party (KPD) in June 1945 to plan the reunification of Germany that under complete Soviet control. This plan was to be achieved by the Soviet Army and the German Communist Party (KPD). Stalin noted to the Yugoslav Communist leaders in the spring of 1946 that *"(A)ll of Germany must be ours…that is, Soviet, Communist."*[3] According to a declassified document, in April 1952, Stalin noted to East German Minister-President Otto Grotewohl that *"You should continue propaganda of German unity in the future. It has a great importance for the education of the people in Western Germany. Now it is a weapon in your hands and you should always hold it in your hands. We should also continue to make proposals regarding German unity in order to expose the Americans."*[4]

Contrary to popular belief, Stalin did not object to German remilitarization as long as it was under the tutelage of the Soviets and their German Communist allies. In November 1942, Stalin noted that *"We do not have such a task as the annihilation of all organized military strength in Germany because any half-literate man can understand that this is in relation to Germany as well as well as in relation to Russia not only impossible, but also, from the standpoint of victor, disadvantageous."*[5]

Even during the darkest days of World War II, the Soviets built the nucleus of a communist-dominated army and political leadership. Every year, approximately 1,000 to 3,000

---

[1] Pincher, Chapman. <u>The Secret Offensive</u> (Sidgwick & Jackson 1986) page 32.
[2] Crozier, Brian. <u>The KGB Lawsuits</u> (Claridge Press 1995) page 229.
[3] Gaddis, John Lewis. <u>We Now Know</u> (Clarendon Press, 1997) page 116.
[4] "Conversation Between Joseph V. Stalin and SED leadership" April 7, 1952 Cold War International History Project Accessed From: http://www.wilsoncenter.org/index.cfm?topic_id=1409&fuseaction=va2.document&identifier=9AD6A331-423B-763D-DBC28A386DF1E71F&sort=Collection&item=Germany%20in%20the%20Cold%20War
[5] Forster, Thomas. <u>The East German Army</u> (Allen & Unwin 1967) pages 16-17.

captured German soldiers and officers were indoctrinated in Antifa (Anti-Fascist) Schools that were run by the Communist Party of Germany (KPD) and the Soviets. The Front Schools provided additional combat training to the captured German POWs, which tended to focus on rear-guard propaganda actions among active Wehrmacht members. These forces were used by the Soviets from about late 1943 to 1945. These Moscow-trained German combat units infiltrated groups of Nazi soldiers who were already surrounded by Soviet forces. Their mission was to attempt *"persuade the besieged troops to surrender, but they were quite willing to fight it out with fanatical Nazi units which tried to prevent their missions. Heavy combat between these Kampfgruppen (Soviet-trained German forces) and resisting Wehrmacht forces took place in Courland as well as at Konigsberg and Breslau."* The United States expressed its displeasure to the Soviets for the activities of the Soviet-created German Officers' League (NKFD) activity in Saxony. Washington was rightfully concerned that Moscow was reviving German militarism under the banner of the Hammer and Sickle.[6]

By 1947, reports reached the West indicating that the Soviets organized *Wehrmacht* POWs into military units to be utilized in a communist Germany. They were commanded by former *Wehrmacht* Generals Friedrich von Paulus, Walter von Seydlitz, Wagner, and Schorner under the rubric of the Soviet-controlled Military Committee for the Renovation of Germany. Thirty six divisions were allegedly developed and equipped with Soviet and ex-German made weapons.[7] Schorner arrived in Tiflis Soviet Georgia with a group of high ranking Soviet generals who were tasked to study the strategic situation in the Near East. Schorner was said to be an observer of the summer maneuvers of Soviet troops in East Germany. Schorner reportedly shared ideas on how the Soviets could launch a Pearl Harbor-style attack on the West in the event of World War III.[8]

As of 1952, 110 former German U-Boat naval officers and seamen passed through Odessa in the Ukraine Soviet Socialist Republic on their way to the Far East. High pay and favorable terms of service were offered as incentives to recruit these ex-*Kriegsmarine* officers and sailors. Some of these ex-*Kriegsmarine* officers worked in submarine repair yards in Vladivostok, while others served on *Kriegsmarine* vessels ceded to the USSR as war reparations.[9]

The Soviets also harnessed the networks of the *Abwehr*, which soon operated with great success in North Africa and the Middle East. This Soviet-controlled Abwehr network was headed by a General Bamler. It was based out of East Berlin and was under the direct control of the Soviets and not the East German military. Bamler recruited former Nazi agents in the Middle East who were recruited on the basis that the Soviets sought to revive German militarism and

---

[6] Smith, Arthur Lee. The War for the German Mind: Re-Educating Hitler's Soldiers (Berghahn Books 1996) pages 117-121.
[7] "Big German Force in Russia Reported" New York Times August 4, 1947 page 3.
[8] Former Nazi Field Marshal Reported in Tiflis with Soviet Generals Radio Free Europe Research Eastern Europe November 13, 1952 Accessed From: http://storage.osaarchivum.org/low/18/9a/189a484d-fb0a-4b2c-87d3-4ad2d1344732_l.pdf
[9] Soviets Reported Recruiting Former U-Boat Crews for the Far East Radio Free Europe Research March 20, 1952 Accessed From: http://storage.osaarchivum.org/low/09/05/09052d69-1fd8-4df3-99d6-bf65e07972c0_l.pdf

power.[10] In fact, Soviet recruitment of entire sections of the Nazi intelligence network was confirmed by other writers and sources. Edward Jay Epstein noted that the Frederick Forsyth novel The Odessa File was *"based on an actual case in which East German intelligence officers assumed the identities of die hard Hitlerites and even created a secret Nazi organization to recruit West German intelligence officers who secretly harbored pro-Nazi sympathies."*[11]

The Soviets and their German collaborators also sought to gather and surreptitiously manufacture weapons for use by communist forces for the consolidation of power in the Eastern/Soviet Zone and the possible push westward. Former German intelligence chief Reinhard Gehlen noted *"While the Soviet Union restocked Hitler's depleted munitions dumps in Eastern Europe, the Western Allies destroyed the arms factories and industrial installations in their zones of Germany."*[12] Allied inspectors based in the Western Zone of Germany were deceived by the Soviets and their German collaborators while on tours of heavy industrial plants in the Soviet Zone of Germany (SBZ). These inspection tours were conducted by the Western Allies to help ensure that the Soviets were not engaged in the remilitarization of their zone in Germany. Count Rudolf von Westarp was the director of the Askania Werke, which was involved in arms manufacturing for the Soviets. Another German Communist official expressed concern to Count von Westarp that the arms making activities at these factories would be discovered by the American occupation authorities who conducted inspections of factories in the Soviet Zone of Germany. Count von Westarp told the German Communist that *"the Americans stick their noses in and then they go off."*[13] Hence, it was implied in von Westarp's statement that the American inspectors were naïve and not entirely committed in terminating or limiting Soviet rearmament efforts in the SBZ.

It was reported that as of August 1946, Russian and German technicians produced V-1 and V-2 at 10 special factories in the SBZ. Other products manufactured at these special plants included torpedo components, special jet aircraft, rocket fuels, and heavy armaments. Plants of the Bleich-Roder concern, Siemens, Telefunken, Nieder-Sachsenwerke, Krupp, and Leuna oil complex produced aircraft fuels and other arms related materials.[14]

According to informants who had connections with a high official of the East German *Volkpolizei* (Vopos), the USSR manufactured ballistic missiles at the ex-Nazi underground plant in Peenemunde. The new rocket was dubbed Fire Lily and its range was 5,000 miles. The facility was guarded by Soviet NKVD forces and surrounded by minefields and high voltage wire. Speedboats also patrolled the area as well.[15]

As of August 1947, the US Military Government in Germany reported that two factories of the Askania Werke produced prohibited war materials. These plants were owned by the Consolidated German Gas Company based in Dessau in the Soviet Zone of Germany. According

---

[10] Soviets Rebuilding Former Nazi Spy Network Radio Free Europe Research Eastern Europe August 28, 1952 Accessed From: http://www.osaarchivum.org/greenfield/repository/osa:2034f319-b6f0-4450-aa63-2a2e578207ce

[11] Epstein, Edward Jay. Deception: The Invisible War Between the KGB and the CIA (Simon & Schuster, 1989) page 303.

[12] Pincher, Chapman. The Secret Offensive (Sidgwick & Jackson 1986) page 14.

[13] "German Weapons Traced to Soviet" New York Times August 3, 1947 page 30.

[14] "Russia Said to Make V-Weapons in Zone" New York Times August 22, 1946 page 2.

[15] "Germans Make New Rocket in Secret Russian Base" The Canberra Times September 28, 1949 page 1.

to American inspectors, goods produced at these plants included gyroscopes, V-1 and V-2 parts, wings, and other aircraft and precision instruments.[16]

As of November 1950, the Soviets paid American dollars to Belgian shipyards in order to repair ex-German merchant marine vessels. These ships included the Hamburg, Cordillera, Hansa, and the ex-Labor Front (DAF) Strength Through Joy ship called Der Deutsche.[17]

The West German Ministry for All-German Affairs noted in May 1951 that the Soviets and East Germany operated *"an armaments program on a great scale."* The report noted that 30 East German factories produced parts for Soviet-made tanks. These plants also produced components for submarines, chassis and tractors for heavy artillery, explosives, searchlights, 450 ton patrol boats, and ammunition. The former German Dye Trust plant in Leuna produced high-yield explosives and jet fuel. Railroad workshops located in Dessau produced flat rail cars to carry heavy guns.[18]

As of July 1950, the area in East Germany around Magdeburg was ringed with factories tasked to produce weapons for the USSR. One company based in Magdeburg was known as the Schaefer & Buddenberg, which manufactured measuring apparatus for artillery. A former German munitions plant near the Elbe River made powder charges for grenades and bullets. In January 1950, a new cellulose plant was constructed in Rothensee, which produced for the armaments sector.[19]

Old Nazis weapons were also transshipped from East Germany to various terrorist and *"national liberation movements."* The Garrisoned Alert Units (KVP) and National People's Army (East German Army) used ex-Nazi STG-44 and MP-40 machine guns. These weapons were then seconded to the Workers' Combat Groups and exported to *"liberation movements"* and terrorists. In the mid-1950s, People's Police officers were also armed with Mauser K98 rifles and STG-44 automatic rifles.[20]

The Soviets were also committed to provide heavy weapons to the paramilitary units of the People's Police in East Germany. The People's Police was intended to be the nucleus of a regular, national army in East Germany. In reference to the creation of a regular army in East Germany, East German President Wilhelm Pieck complained to Stalin that the People's Police *"police are poorly armed, have bad revolvers that lack bullets."* Stalin responded to Pieck's assertion *"what kind of police is that?"* Stalin noted to Pieck that *"the GDR can produce their own machine guns, rifles, revolvers and bullets for the People's Police. You have the full right to do it."* Stalin also remarked to Pieck that *"you need to create an army."*[21]

---

[16] Raymond, Jack. "Armaments Made in 2 Berlin Plants" New York Times August 2, 1947 page 1.

[17] McLaughlin, Kathleen. "Sunk German Ships Raised for Soviet" New York Times November 11, 1950 page 21.

[18] "East German Shops Said to Make Arms" New York Times May 30, 1951 page 7.

[19] McLaughlin, Kathleen. "Soviet Zone Units Making War Goods" New York Times July 2, 1950 page 5.

[20] Accessed From: http://forum.axishistory.com/viewtopic.php?f=60&t=57447

[21] "Conversations between Joseph V. Stalin and SED leadership" April 1, 1952 Cold War International History Project Accessed From: http://www.wilsoncenter.org/index.cfm?topic_id=1409&fuseaction=va2.document&identifier=5034FD88-96B6-175C-93105576DC034850&sort=Collection&item=Stalin%20and%20the%20Cold%20War

The East German People's Police and later the National People's Army (NVA) were to be tasked by the Soviets and the ruling communist party in East Germany (the Socialist Unity Party or SED) to conquer West Germany and install a puppet regime in Bonn. The Soviets and the SED would garner several benefits from a conquered West Germany. Undamaged factories and technology would pass into the hands on the communists. Moscow and East Berlin would also gain a springboard to attack other Western countries. East German intentions to conquer West Germany were made very clear early on. SED Secretary Walter Ulbricht noted in 1952 that *"Our national forces will be the army of the people of the German Democratic Republic, now that they have been liberated from imperialism. The creation of national forces will give the people's movement in Western Germany a stronger hold and more courage in their struggle against Adenauer."* The Thalmann Song that was written by the poet Kurt Bartels had the following stanza: *"Dream build! And forward we go-The Rhine shall our own freedom share. Break off the claws of the foe: Thalmann will always be there."* Lt Col Schmidt, writing in the Lausitzer Rundschau, noted *"The German Democratic Republic is the westernmost outpost of socialism. It is our task to help socialism to a breakthrough in the West."*[22]

Gotz Scharf wrote in his 1959 book On The Moral Factor in the Modern War that *"Through the body and blood of every member of the NPA must penetrate the realization that every soldier of NATO, even if he is of German origin, who raises arms against the socialist camp, is not his brother but his foe. Our brothers in West Germany are the patriots fighting under the leadership of the illegal Communist Party of Germany…"*[23]

Army General Heinz Hoffmann noted in a 1975 lecture called The Armed Forces In Our Time that the NVA was important in fulfilling the *"spreading of socialism/communism throughout the world…So far in truth history has witnessed no case in which a socialist revolution was led to victory without the guns speaking their message of power-or at least being aimed and loaded."*[24]

Usage of the East German People's Police and later the National People's Army in the invasion and occupation of West Germany was confirmed by defectors. In 1949, defecting People's Police Major General Walter Schreiber noted that the organization he helped command was *"really is a new army being readied on the orders of the Kremlin for the Sovietization of the Western Zones of the Reich as soon as the moment is ripe."* Schreiber noted further that the People's Police had the duty to fulfill its *"historical mission of unifying Germany…this time under the Red Flag."* Significantly, Schreiber also reported that after all of Germany was communized, the Soviets and Germans would then *"make their next move to the (English) Channel."*[25]

An official SED organization called the Free German Youth (FDJ) was also publicly delegated with the task of assisting the Soviet Army in an attack and occupation of West Germany. In 1950, the FDJ issued a statement that asserted: *"The members and officials of the FDJ must make it clear to the population, especially the youth, that in case of a new aggression*

---

[22] US Army Military History Institute. The Total Militarisation of the Soviet Occupied Zone of Germany (Celle/Hannover, Germany: Pohl Publishing House, 1960) pages 19-22.
[23] Forster, Thomas. The East German Army (Allen & Unwin 1967) pages 156-157.
[24] Forster, Thomas. The East German Army: the Second Power in the Warsaw Pact (Allen & Unwin 1980) page 29.
[25] Schreiber, Walter. "People's Police in Reich Army Aid Conquering" Post Standard April 14, 1949 page 7.

it is the duty of the German people and the youth to fight against the aggressors and to support the Soviet Army in bringing peace."[26]

A defecting lieutenant from the Volkspolizei (People's Police) revealed in 1951 that the Soviets trained 600 ardent communists to serve as battalion commanders of the future East German army and junior officers in the Bereitschaften (Alert Forces-militarized police). The secret school was located in Kochstedt near Dessau. Trainees were informed that they would serve alongside Soviet forces in case there was an attack against East Germany. However, the lieutenant believed that the East would attack the West, with the Soviet Army as the main attacking force. The Bereitschaften would serve as *"hangers on"* that would fight under Soviet command.[27]

In 1956, NATO military authorities noted that East German National People's Army troops would be utilized during a conflict with the West for communications and internal security functions for Soviet forces. These sources reported that token East German units would be used in the invasion of the West to give a *"liberation color to the aggression."*[28]

Defecting East German Army Captain Guenther Malikowski of the First Motorized Rifle Division in Potsdam noted that the communist indoctrination within the military focused on East Germany's *"justified war of liberation"* against West Germany. East German troops were ordered to show no mercy in the battle with the West Germans and NATO forces. Furthermore, they were instructed to kill fellow Germans if they were found aiding the *"imperialist"* cause. East German Army Captain Eduard Wedmann, a former artillery officer in the Eighth Motorized Rifle Division in Schwerin, recalled that *"recent East German military exercises presuppose an invasion of West Germany using nuclear weapons at the outset, without regard to whether West Germany has used them first...We have no nuclear weapons now, but when they are needed, they will be available."*[29]

When Malikowski defected, he carried samples of East German military documents and propaganda leaflets that were crafted purposely to win over the West German population during an East German and Soviet occupation. The leaflets were intended for West German citizens and West German Army (Bundeswehr) personnel to turn against the government and join the communist occupation. The East Germans also printed passes for West Germans to defect and cross into East German-held territory. One leaflet addressed *"German brothers"* and implored that *"The Adenauer*[30] *era is over. Do not go down with it."* Another addressed the citizens of Kiel by stating: *"The last pockets of resistance in the city have been wiped out. The city is in the hands of the troops of the National People's Army of the German Democratic Republic. The army of the first workers' and farmers' state in Germany has not come as an occupation army to tyrannize over the working people. We have come to do away with fascism and militarism in Germany once and for all. We seek the cooperation of the democratically minded and*

---

[26] "Soviet Army Aid Held East Germans' Duty" <u>New York Times</u> June 19, 1950 page 4.

[27] De Luce, Daniel. "Secret War College Revealed" <u>Lubbock Morning Avalanche</u> August 28, 1951 pages 1 and 20.

[28] Olsen, Arthur J. "West Minimizing Red German Army" <u>New York Times</u> February 16, 1956 page 3.

[29] "Russia: Temperature Control" <u>Time Magazine</u> November 7, 1960 Accessed From: http://www.time.com/time/magazine/article/0,9171,826690,00.html

[30] Konrad Adenauer was the first Federal Chancellor of West Germany. He represented the Christian Democratic Party (CDU) in West Germany.

constructive forces of the city." Each document indicated the total numbers printed and the method of delivery. These leaflets were also marked *"Strictly Confidential! Internal Party Material."*[31]

In 1962, Lt. Col. Martin Herbert Loeffler defected and reported that he studied military science problems that focused on themes related to the territory of West Germany. Loeffler noted that: *"he himself worked out a problem for the conquest of the Ruhr industrial area of West Germany. In connection with this, detailed attention was paid to the number of atomic weapons to be used in order to paralyze the area."* He noted that the Soviets would first send the six divisions which comprised the East German National People's Army to invade West Germany. Loeffler also believed that most of the soldiers in his regiment would fight the West if called into battle.[32]

Belgian General Robert Close noted in 1976 that a Soviet and Warsaw Pact invasion and the subsequent defeat of West Germany could be achieved in forty eight hours.[33] Close noted that speed and flexibility would have been the key ingredients to Soviet successes in a future battle against NATO. The Soviet helicopter fleet would have provided tremendous transport capacity for troops. NATO installations, bridges crossing the Rhine River, and army barracks would have been targets from helicopter borne troop assaults. Fifth column activities would work in tandem with these helicopter assaults to cripple West Germany. Close estimated that 15,000 to 20,000 Soviet agents were employed in West Germany. Their targets were telecommunications, radio and television stations, NATO Headquarters, nuclear depots, early warning radars, and high ranking officials.[34]

The invasion and occupation plans for West Berlin and Germany were codenamed by the East Germans Operation Stoss and after 1987, Operation Zentrum (Center). These operations would involve 32,000 Stasi, People's Police, elite airborne units (e.g. Willi Sanger paratroop units) and regular East German and Soviet army units.[35] Intelligence Digest reported in 1978 that Moscow would create a situation where an *"East German anti-Nazi police action"* would result in an all-out Soviet invasion of West Germany.[36] Even during the period of *"glasnost"* and *"perestroika,"* East Germany continued to formulate attack plans against West Germany. In 1988, Stasi chief Erich Mielke informed a grouping of Stasi officers that World War III would *"commence with an attack of the Warsaw Pact forces on the Federal Republic (West Germany)."*[37]

It was reported in the late 1960s that the East German newspaper Neues Deutschland predicted that a conventional battle in Europe would descend into a nuclear conflict *"from the very beginning or within a few days."* The article also called for the intensive training of East

---

[31] "East German Army Preparing to Invade Federal Republic" Times (London) September 16, 1960 page 8.
[32] "East German Colonel Predicts Berlin Blockade" Stars and Stripes September 22, 1962 page 24.
[33] Close, Robert. Europe Without Defense? (Pergamon Press: New York 1979) page 177.
[34] Ibid, pages 180-184.
[35] Wenzel, Dr. Otto. "East German Plans for the Conquest and Occupation of West Berlin" Armor November-December 1994 page 7.
[36] Intelligence Digest Intelligence International Ltd., 1978 page 2.
[37] Koehler, Bernard. Stasi: The Untold Story of the East German Secret Police (Basic Books 2008) page 28.

German forces in nuclear and missile tactics, along with a general mobilization of the East German population for a world war. The East Germans were told that they were to fight their *"West German brothers"* and stand on the side of the USSR in the event of a West German attack on the East. The conflict would then become in Soviet and East German eyes a *"just national"* war for *"the liberation of West Germany."*[38] Even during the time of détente, the East German political leadership and top military commanders sought a victory over the West through the usage of nuclear weapons. In a 1976 lecture in East Berlin, General Heinz Hoffmann noted that *"We do not share…the view expressed even by progressive people in the peace movement that a just war is no longer possible in the atomic age or that a war waged with nuclear missiles would be a mere atomic inferno and the end of the world rather than a continuation of the policies of the struggling classes."*[39]

Despite the misinterpretation of détente as a relaxation in tensions, the Soviets and their allies continued to increase their war preparations. Détente was an opportunity for Moscow and East Berlin to build up their armed forces and lull the West into a sense of complacency in respect to the threat of international communism. The East Germans followed their Soviet allies in viewing détente as an opportunity to push forward the class struggle against the capitalist world. In 1978, the NVA publication <u>Militarwesen</u> noted that *"Certain bourgeois politicians express amazement and alarm at the solidarity of shown by Soviet communists and the Soviet people with the struggles of other nations for freedom and progress. This is either naiveté or more likely a deliberate effort to confuse people's minds…Détente however in no way eliminates or changes the laws of class struggle…We make no secret of our opinions…In the Party's view détente does not and cannot mean a freezing of the objective processes of historical evolution."* The article also noted that peaceful coexistence was *"a particular form of class struggle between socialism and capitalism"* which was to create favorable conditions *"for the international proletariat's fight to destroy imperialism and for the revolutionary transformation of society."*[40]

Studies concluded that the East German army would have fought against their West German compatriots in the Bundeswehr. While defections to NATO were expected, the East German troops and officers were sufficiently indoctrinated and it was believed that their troops would have fought loyally to achieve a reunified communist Germany. While the Bundeswehr was stripped of Germany's Prussian military culture, the East Germans retained such trappings within its armed forces. A German ex-officer observed the differences between the East and West German armies when he stated *"Both are going to be well-trained, because their respective backers want it that way. But the East Germans have been given a military tradition which they can more easily understand. Both armies must pay for most of their weapons. But the East Germans will not waste time arguing about theirs; they will merely be equipped by the Russians. Both armies will be reluctant to fire on fellow Germans. But the East Germans have already had practice in doing this, in June 1953. The West Germans are being trained to take part in the defense of the West, but the East Germans are just being trained to carry out orders. West Germans are being taught that they have no traditional foes; East Germans are being filled brimful with vitriolic invective directed against 'Western and NATO militarists and warmongers!' They are learning that they are the 'new Prussians,' standing guard against the*

---

[38] "A-War Stressed by German Reds" <u>New York Times</u> November 24, 1968 page 19.
[39] Forster, Thomas. <u>The East German Army: the Second Power in the Warsaw Pact</u> (Allen & Unwin 1980) page 30.
[40] Ibid, page 36.

decadent, plutocratic but acquisitive West. It is they who will recapture a composite Germanic spirit of aggression and blind obedience; and it is they who may constitute a danger to the peace of Central Europe."[41]

One East German officer noted *"It may perhaps sound ironic from our present point of view, since we are in the West and not in the GDR. However in the event of a military confrontation I believe that the hate cultivated against the West and the Bundeswehr will bring results. I would warn you against underestimating this problem. There will be shooting; nobody in the NPA would say, 'Those people are Germans.' They will fight; I am totally convinced of this. There will be people who will desert. However, one has to look at the system as a whole and I am convinced that the NPA will fight. In terms of the purely military situation, when the commander stands behind me, I have to shoot. In terms of the psychological aspect of it, the soldier on the other side is a soldier of the Bundeswehr. That is of no interest to me at all. Again I would like to warn anybody who says 'Well it's not going to be so bad, the National People's Army would think it over and would not shoot at its brothers and sisters.'"*[42]

An East German border guard recollected: *"We were told, 'We won't give up a centimeter of territory.' That could only mean that we must launch an attack."* East German border guards were taught *"We must observe war preparations. If the Bundeswehr is in the stage of planning an attack, we must act then."*

A defecting East German officer warned: *"The combat readiness and reliability of the East German Army are often underestimated...I would like to emphasize quite strongly that in case of a successful blitzkrieg there would be no problems. Myths from the Third Reich also come into play. They are not as dead as one sometimes thinks, at least as far as the NPA is concerned."*[43]

A good indicator of the willingness of Soviet and East German forces to kill Americans was the relationship with the US Military Liaison Mission (USMLM) based in East Germany. Until the 1974 opening of the US Embassy in East Berlin, the USMLM Mission in Potsdam was the only official American presence in East Germany.[44] The British also maintained a liaison mission known as BRIXMIS, which also faced similar forms of harassment and attacks.

The survival of the USMLM was dependent on East German and Soviet services and materials. The Potsdam House of the USMLM employed 9 East German staff which consisted of four cooks/waitresses, 3 cleaning women, 1 gardener, and one mechanic. The Soviets provided coal, rations, trash pickup, utilities, gasoline, and telephone service. East German police and guard forces provided 24 hour *"security"* for the Potsdam House.[45] The Stasi and KGB also monitored BRIXMIS and the USMLM. The East German Staff at Mission House in Potsdam were Stasi agents, according to Fahey. He noted that Siegfried a member of the House staff was a *"top Stasi agent"* and who was *"a most adept master spy who possessed a special gift that*

---

[41] Prittie, Terence. Germany Divided: The Legacy of the Nazi Era (Literary Licensing, LLC, 2012) pages 186-187.
[42] Johnson, A. Ross; Dean, Robert W.; and Alexiev, Alexander. East European Military Establishments (Crane, Russak, 1982) page 120.
[43] Alexiev, Alexander and Johnson, A. Ross. East European Military Reliability(RAND Corporation, 1986) Accessed From: http://www.rand.org/content/dam/rand/pubs/reports/2006/R3480.pdf
[44] Holbrook, James R. Potsdam Mission (AuthorHouse, 2008) page 13.
[45] Ibid, page 19.

enabled him to be beloved by the easy victims of his intelligence collection."[46] A BRIXMIS handler noted that *"in essence, all Mission House staff members were being run by either the MfS or the KGB to varying degrees of success as a precondition of continued employment. Handling rights were being worked out between the KGB and the MfS Commanding Officer at Beyerstrasse, Potsdam, on a fifty-fifty basis."*[47] One former BRIXMIS officer who was stationed in East Germany noted that *"We also worked on the assumption that all the other locally employed staff members were under the control of the Stasi authorities."*[48]

Since the USMLM House in Potsdam was the only official US presence in pre-1974 East Germany, it invited anti-American violence. In July 1958, after the Suez Crisis, hundreds of East Germans stormed the British Liaison Mission (BRIXMIS) and Potsdam Houses. In June 1965, East German anti-Vietnam War protestors assaulted the Potsdam House and tore down the US flag and ransacked the mansion. Some of the *"students"* removed a US flag and painted the slogan *"Ami go home."*[49]

Between 1962 and 1990, there were 49 shooting incidents involving USMLM teams. In 1966, a USMLM tour vehicle was machine gunned. In 1962, a BRIXMIS corporal was wounded in a gun attack by East Germans. Between 1979 and 1985, BRIXMIS crews were rammed and detained 25 times and subjected to four shootings by East German and Soviet forces. In 1959, a USMLM team was beaten up in a hotel room in Karl Marx Stadt by East German State Security squads. The East Germans also robbed their possessions and broke into their car. In March 1979, a large Czechoslovak-built Tatra-813 trucked purposely rammed into a USMLM car. Soviet personnel then broke into the damaged car. A Soviet general threatened the Chief of USMLM that USMLM teams *"might collide with a tank or a big truck."* In June 1965, an East German spokesman noted that the USMLM should leave East Germany since it was *"an unnecessary holdover of postwar occupation."*[50]

East German State Security (Stasi) agents tailed USMLM cars with a variety of vehicles. Stasi squads used American-built Buicks, East German Wartburgs, West German-made Mercedes and BMWs, and Soviet-built Ladas, Volgas, and Moskvichs.[51] The Stasi reportedly acquired these American-made cars by stealing them in Munich.[52] The Stasi were also aided by the Border Police, People's Police, Alert Police, Railway Police, business managers, foresters, political officials, and so called *"do-gooder citizens."*[53]

From its earliest days, the East Germans sought to create sabotage forces for the purpose of crippling crucial West German industries, infrastructure, and the political leadership. As of 1953, the East German Ministry of the Interior was ordered by the Soviet Control Commission to create 6 special schools in East Germany for the training of *"resistance fighters"* to battle against the West German government. Trainees were nominated by the ruling Socialist Unity Party

---

[46] Fahey, John A. Licensed to Spy (Naval Institute Press, 2002) pages 22, 146.
[47] Geraghty, Tony. Beyond the frontline: the untold exploits of Britain's most daring Cold War spy mission (HarperCollins, 1996)
[48] Accessed From: http://kms2.isn.ethz.ch/serviceengine/Files/.../BRIXMIS_1980s.pdf
[49] Holbrook, James R. Potsdam Mission (AuthorHouse, 2008) page 19.
[50] Ibid, page 31.
[51] Ibid, page 172.
[52] Nikulla, Paul. "Air Team USMLM" Accessed From: www.berlin6912.org/publications/Nikulla2.doc
[53] Holbrook, James R. Potsdam Mission (AuthorHouse, 2008) page 171.

(SED), the official Free German Trade Union (FDGB), and the Free German Youth (FDJ). The schools were located at People's Police barracks. The training covered such subjects as the tactics of the US Army and street fighting with firearms, acts of sabotage, and courses in the English language.[54]

In June 1951, the East Germans trained a large number of agents from both zones to sabotage West German defense efforts and participation in NATO. This force was separate from other East German intelligence services and the manpower consisted of ex-Wehrmacht officers. They were trained under the tutelage of communist military and propaganda specialists and entered FDJ training camps. The recruitment of these former Wehrmacht troops and officers commenced after the Soviet-controlled World Youth Festival was held in East Berlin, which was also when anti-militarist agents traveled from West Germany. These West Germans were trained in secret FDJ camps and then infiltrated back into West Germany to enter the Bundeswehr in order to carry out propaganda and sabotage. These secret agents were to spread defeatist, pacifist, and anti-American propaganda among circles within the West German Army; disrupt the morale and criticize the officers; criticize the conditions of service and food; and encourage the surrender of West German Army units in the event of a Soviet invasion. These infiltrators were promised commissions in the East German People's Police and large sums of money.[55]

In 1951, a group of specially selected FDJ functionaries attended Soviet Ministry of State Security (MGB) training courses in Leningrad. West German communist youth were forged into crack sabotage units at this school. These 19-21 year old trainees would then be dispatched to West Germany under the guise of refugees and subsequently blended into society and be activated in an emergency.[56]

Sleepers were trained at the Franz Mehring Institute in East Berlin for 1 year courses. The Ernst Thalmann School in Schmerwitz trained working men's commandos that were also known as Techno Kommandos. Graduates were set up with jobs in West Germany under cover identities who would then conduct sabotage upon activation in wartime. The Grenzaufklarer (Border Reconnaissance) troops were controlled by the East German Ministry for State Security (MfS). They photographed Western forces that were stationed on the other side of the Inter-German (East/West German) border. These Border Reconnaissance forces were also tasked with sabotage during wartime.[57]

A former Chief of the Rhine Army noted that at least 400 subversion units existed in West Germany. The total number of subversive sleepers in West Germany was 20,000 agents who operated in the guise of refugees and students.[58]

During the 1950s, the Stasi first formed a unit of sabotage troops in West Germany. In the event of World War III, they were tasked for activation. These Stasi sabotage troops served

---

[54] "Sabotage Training in East Germany" Radio Free Europe Research Eastern Europe March 28, 1953 Accessed From: http://storage.osaarchivum.org/low/4d/13/4d132a2e-4695-4b2a-bcac-9234e54bf8f1_1.pdf

[55] "Eastern Germany" Radio Free Europe Research Eastern Europe February 23, 1952 Accessed From: http://storage.osaarchivum.org/low/43/7b/437b01ce-dd21-4d4a-b783-3b266f741761_1.pdf

[56] "Eastern Germany" Radio Free Europe Research Eastern Europe September 26, 1951 Accessed From: http://storage.osaarchivum.org/low/ab/7d/ab7dafad-c5fd-423d-ad98-f6db3446bfb0_1.pdf

[57] Welham, Michael G. and Quarrie, Bruce. Operation Spetsnaz (P. Stephens, 1989) pages 45-46.

[58] Pincher, Chapman. The Secret Offensive (Sidgwick & Jackson 1986) page 254.

as a partner of the KGB Administration V of the Main Directorate. It was known as the Minister's Working Group (AGM/S) and was further expanded in the 1970s. The AGM/S maintained 300 troops by the end of the 1970s. In 1981, the AGM/S was assigned 346 designated civil and military targets in West Germany. As of the early 1960s, the AGM/S also employed 86 unofficial collaborators in West Germany. The AGM/S maintained stores of firearms and West German Deutschemarks at their disposal. In 1968, it was supplemented by 200 members of a secret military organization of the West German Communist Party (DKP). The AGM/S was supposed to carry out *"physical operations"* in times of peace. Under agreements with the KGB, these operations were to occur *"under the respective national flag or third hand, with consistent veiling of one's own participation"* using the weapons and equipment of the enemy.[59]

In specific terms, the Stasi's AGM/S – *"Minister Working Group/Special Operations"* was responsible for *"intimidating anti-communist opinion leaders"* by *"liquidation,"* and *"kidnapping or hostage taking, connected with the demand that political messages be read."*[60]

The East Germans also maintained an elite force of 3,000 *"partisan comrades"* that were commissioned to create chaos and terror in Western Europe in the event of World War III. This force was created by East Germany in the 1960s and was known as Department IV. One former member of this commando force named Siegfried Mann noted *"We were the comrades given the task of helping freedom movements in the West, especially the terrorists and revolutionaries…We taught them and helped them. We were softening up western imperialism from the inside ready for a communist takeover."*[61]

The 3,000 *"partisan comrades"* of Department IV were responsible for destroying power plants, big business, broadcasting stations, armaments factories, and government offices. The Stasi also relied on 30,000 *"informal members"* in West Germany and the rest of Western Europe to assist them in their activities, including sabotage in the event of World War III. One such *"informal member"* code-named Jupp stole a large number of American Army uniforms and passed them on to the East German Stasi. The East Germans used these uniforms to create a unit which disguised themselves as American soldiers and officers in West Germany.[62]

In southern East Germany, a special diversionary battalion of the Stasi was equipped with US-made M-113 APCs and M-48 tanks which were obtained from communist Vietnam after the collapse of the South Vietnamese army and government. These armored vehicles were painted with West German Army markings and the Stasi troops were dressed like West German soldiers. They would be used for unconventional warfare duties behind NATO lines and were under the command of the MfS.[63]

---

[59] Gieseke, Jens. "East German Espionage in the Era of Détente" Journal of Strategic Studies June 2008 pages 405-408.
[60] Crawford, David. "The Murder of a CEO: Did East Germany's Feared Secret Police Help Kill German Businessmen?" September 15, 2007 Accessed From: http://online.wsj.com/public/article_print/SB118981435771628219.html
[61] Michael Woodhead. "Stasi Spy Files Reveal Secret Hit Squad: High-Tech Assassination Team Operated Until Fall of Berlin Wall in 1989" The Ottawa Citizen May 09, 1999 page A11.
[62] Woodhead, Michael. "How Stasi Spies Won Licence to Kill" Sunday Times May 9, 1999
[63] Zaloga, Steven J. and Loop, James. Soviet Bloc Elite Forces (Osprey Publishing, 1985) pages 50-54.

Commando forces of East Germany and Poland were in possession of Danish army uniforms that were to be used in infiltration activities before a Third World War erupted. There were 15 Soviet Spetsnaz training and command centers in the Baltic area that maintained ties to the Baltic Fleet. Furthermore, these Spetsnaz troops were assigned targets in Denmark, West Germany, and Sweden. East German soldiers also possessed West German police uniforms which were to be worn during the infiltration process shortly before a Third World War erupted in Europe. Local Spetsnaz contacts included local agents from various extreme leftist elements in the targeted countries. These leftists would provide Spetsnaz agents with safe houses and even engage in minor acts of sabotage.[64]

The National People's Army possessed a paratroop unit which was formed in 1962 and was known as Paratroop Battalion 40. It was known as the Willi Saenger Battalion and consisted of 400-500 men. It was based Prora on the Baltic Island of Ruegen. The Willi Saenger Battalion were charged with missions to destroy nuclear weapons carriers, enemy command organs, and destroy enemy supplies. Paratroops were to be dropped from AN-2 and AN-14 transport planes over enemy territory. These troops were also tasked with the following assignments: commando operations against enemy military installation while dressed in NATO uniforms; direction and support of already existing underground forces and gangs; abduction of enemy VIPs; and creation of chaos in NATO rear areas and surprise attacks and provocations. An example of such an operation would be East German troops disguised as Bundeswehr troops attacking American installations. According to a top Warsaw Pact military planner, the Czechoslovak Major General Jan Sejna, Operation Dunaj would partially entail the usage of the paratroopers of the National People's Army to attack targets of high strategic importance in West Germany. They were to seize these targets at the beginning of the assault operations after reaching the operational areas via airdrop.[65]

A former member of the British Special Boat Squadron rated the Willi Sanger Battalion *"the best operational airborne unit in training and active service within the SovBloc countries."* According to East German defector Rainer Paul Fuller, the Battalion trained at the Edgar-Andrae Ausbildungszentrale in Lehnin near the Berlin-Dessau railways. The Willi Sanger Battalion shared this camp with the East German Foreign Intelligence (HVA), who were largely responsible for infiltrating agents and sleepers into West Germany. The NVA Paratroopers' Handbook noted *"Before the deployment of the LL paratroops the commander can obtain addresses of responsible persons who can support them. Care must be taken, the area observed and secured and the password asked for carefully. Encounters can be organized for the paratroops to meet with guerrilla units."*[66]

The East German border forces also contained units of the Grenzaufklarungszug (GAKs), which were formed in the early 1970s. These were special frontier reconnaissance forces which were organized into squad or platoon sized units. GAK troops operated on the western side of the Grenze fences and were expected to operate as guerrillas in case of a war. The GAKs were

---

[64] "Denmark's Defense Minister: Polish, GDR Troops in Danish Uniforms" Berlingske Tidende September 15, 1985

[65] Neuer, Capt. Reinhold. "Structure, Deployment of Paratroop Forces Detailed" Bonn Truppenpraxis July 1983

[66] Welham, Michael G. and Quarrie, Bruce. Operation Spetsnaz (P. Stephens, 1989) pages 43-44.

supposed to make contact with Stasi agents and East German/Soviet sympathizers in West Germany.[67]

The East Germans constructed underground tunnels near the West German border towns of Ratzeburg and Luebeck in Northern Germany and in Bavaria. The exits were disguised as holes in the ground. The East Germans slipped border guard reconnaissance patrols and Stasi agents through these tunnels into West Germany for intelligence purposes. These reconnaissance troops of the border guard were comprised of loyal communists who rarely defected to the West.[68]

The two forty-meter long tunnels that ran under the East German metal border fence between Thuringen and Bayern were used for Stasi agents who shepherded intelligence agents and leftist terrorists into West Germany. They were also believed to serve as transit routes for East German border troops which pursued defectors to West Germany.[69]

Air travel was also used by the East Germans to infiltrate its agents and possibly sabotage forces in foreign countries. As of the early 1970s, Berlin Schonefeld International Airport maintained air connections to Moscow and other East Bloc cities, Amsterdam, Vienna, Copenhagen, Milan, and Stockholm. Planes leaving for Western destinations were *"packed with HVA agents."* Vienna was a favored and convenient destination for these HVA agents and the Austrian authorities proved to be of little hindrance to the movement of East Berlin's intelligence services.[70]

Sabotage groups from the USSR and the Soviet Bloc that were stationed in West Germany were reportedly comprised of five to six members. Furthermore, these East German sabotage groups were to be joined by accomplices in the native country via orders transmitted on radios. The saboteurs wore civilian clothing to disguise their true nature. During the initial stages of the operation, the sabotage forces were to only carry light weapons. The equipment that they were to use was located in caches within the vicinity of the target. The accomplices of these East German sabotage forces included legal residents (i.e. employees of embassies, consulates, airlines, travel agencies, and news agencies) in the target countries. There were 170 legal residences of the KGB in West Germany as of 1978. The Soviet Military Missions in Frankfurt/Main, Buende, and in Baden-Baden also monitored and provided information on targets such as NATO ammunition dumps, dams, and troop movements.[71]

Various avenues for trade and commerce were used by East German and other European satellites to collect intelligence and plant saboteurs in West Germany and elsewhere. East German TIR trucks of the state enterprise VEB Deutrans carried signal monitoring equipment and espionage personnel under the guise of international trade within Europe.[72] Three thousand Deutrans trucks transited West Germany on a monthly basis.[73] These trucks were not subjected to the usual customs checks and were allowed to carry their cargoes. In 1980, Soviet KGB

---

[67] Rottman, Gordon L. The Berlin Wall (Osprey Publishing, 2008) pages 53-55.
[68] "International" United Press International October 6, 1983
[69] Wolfe, Nancy Travis. Policing a Socialist Society: The German Democratic Republic (Greenwood Press, 1992) pages 62-63.
[70] Stiller, Werner. Beyond the Wall (Brassey's (US), 1992) pages 127-128.
[71] "Details of Soviet Bloc Sabotage Missions Revealed" Die Welt August 11, 1978
[72] Rottman, Gordon L. The Berlin Wall (Osprey Publishing, 2008) pages 53-54.
[73] "High-Ranking East German Leads Police To Alleged Spy" The Associated Press March 18, 1988

defector Ilya Dzhirkvelov reported that *"All Soviet truck drivers and co-drivers on West German roads are by profession tank commanders and officers of the Red Army. They are gathering information on every road, street, and bridge."* In 1987, a British intelligence officer based in West Germany reported that Soviet and Eastern Bloc truck traffic on West German roads increased during major NATO exercises in West Germany and The Netherlands. East German, Czechoslovak, Polish, and Hungarian Lada and Skoda cars also flooded the West, while a trickle of Western trucks and cars plied the roads and highways in the East. One East German truck was parked near an American Army base in Stuttgart in 1984, where an accidental fire burned and revealed sensitive and highly sophisticated eavesdropping equipment that could pick up impulses of electric typewriters on the base.[74] The East German merchant marine and fishing fleets were also utilized for similar intelligence operations.[75]

The East Germans also clearly abused the spirit of the goodwill fostered by open diplomacy when they used their Permanent Mission in Bonn to help spruce up the image of the SED regime, launch influence operations in West Germany, and to gather intelligence. The East German Permanent Mission in Bonn and the Trade Mission in Dusseldorf were utilized by the East German Foreign Intelligence (HVA) HA-III for (Signals Intelligence) SIGINT operations.[76]

The fortress-like Permanent Mission of the German Democratic Republic in Bonn West Germany was guarded with highly sensitive video cameras, sealed off with electronic barriers, and whose windows had the blinds drawn down in order to obscure the general mischief performed inside the building. One report described the Mission as *"a cleverly camouflaged espionage and smuggling center of the SED and Stasi."* The Mission maintained a gigantic antenna used to monitor radio traffic and telephone conversations in Bonn. Once or twice a month a small bus from the Mission would travel to East Berlin with packages disguised as diplomatic mail. In reality, this *"diplomatic mail"* consisted of high technology equipment that was prohibited by COCOM. Non-coded and secret coded radio messages from the West German intelligence, Foreign Ministry, and other diplomatic missions were sent via the Mission to the Stasi based in East Berlin.[77]

The HVA's Main Department III operated electronic monitoring facilities from Soviet and East German embassies and missions in Bonn, Cologne, Dusseldorf, Vienna, and Brussels.[78] HA III/Department 9 was responsible for maintaining East German electronic intelligence monitoring sites outside of the GDR. HA III/Department 9 collaborated closely with the Stasi and with Czechoslovak intelligence. One such HA III/Department 9 site was the East German Permanent Mission in Bonn. The Mission was equipped with 35 tape recorders and 32 receivers which operated 24 hours a day. HA III agents at the Mission spied on the Office for the Protection of the Constitution (BfV), the West German intelligence (BND), the Bundeswehr

---

[74] Welham, Michael G. and Quarrie, Bruce. <u>Operation Spetsnaz</u> (P. Stephens, 1989) pages 99-100.
[75] Fischer, Ben. "One of the Biggest Ears in the World: East German SIGINT Operations" Accessed From: http://berndpulch.files.wordpress.com/2012/03/east-german-sigint-operations.pdf
[76] Ibid.
[77] "Permanent Mission in Bonn Seen As Spy Center" <u>Hamburg Bild Am Sonntag</u> August 19, 1990
[78] Gieseke, Jens. "East German Espionage in the Era of Détente" <u>Journal of Strategic Studies</u> June 2008 pages 405-408.

counterintelligence (MAD), and the microwave network for mobile telephones of the Federal Post Office. In 1982, a HA III site in Cologne had a special antenna that intercepted microwave transmissions from the headquarters of the British Army of the Rhine and NATO microwave transmissions to stations such as in Bonn, Oslo, The Hague, Copenhagen, and Brussels.[79]

The Soviets and the East Germans also intended to utilize the West German Communist Party (DKP) as a sabotage force as well. Selected DKP cadres were to be mobilized in the event of a Soviet invasion of West Germany. The American High Commissioner in West Germany John J. McCloy noted in 1951 that his administration received intelligence that *"Communist leaders in western Germany are 'indicating' to the party's inner circle that a Soviet attack may come any time 'this year or next or the year after.' 'When Red troops move westward, the faithful are told, party workers must be ready to perform allotted tasks of sabotage, erect road blocks, conduct partisan warfare and spot targets.' 'Communist party leaders in western Germany are intent upon imparting a sense of immediacy to trusted party workers.'"*[80]

The defecting Stasi officer Werner Stiller also recalled that the DKP in West Germany assisted MfS agents and was assigned to serve as a *"fifth column"* in the event of a direct attack on West Germany. The DKP existed under orders from the SED Central Committee and the MfS.[81] The West German Communist Party (DKP) dispatched cadres to East Germany for military training in sabotage, industrial unrest, and protests that were supposed to flare up during a Warsaw Pact invasion.[82] Stasi General Alexander Schalck-Golodkowski provided $91 million to the DKP underground commando force from 1985 to 1989. This money came from the accounts of the SED. The commando force totaled 300 troops.[83]

During the entire period of the open Cold War, East Germany was delegated with the major task of providing massive assistance in *"liberating"* West Germany and occupying that nation alongside other Warsaw Pact and Soviet troops. The Soviets and East Germans sought to absorb West Berlin into East Berlin, which was the capital of East Germany. Izvestiya noted on November 28, 1958 that *"Berlin should be united with the Eastern Sector and then Berlin would become a single city, belonging to that government in the territory of which it lies."*[84]

The invading Soviets and East Germans also possessed specific lists as to who to liquidate in West German society, politics, and business. The 3,000 *"partisan comrades"* of Department IV had a list of more than 1,000 prominent Westerners for execution. They included leading members of the West German government. This list included even leftist SPD officials Willy Brandt and Helmut Schmidt, who were architects of *Ostpolitik* and further concessions to East Germany, the USSR, and other communist nations. Perhaps the East Germans considered even these SPD luminaries to be potential enemies. One source noted that *"Gerhard Schroder,*

---

[79] "The MfS's Operations in the West: The Interaction of "Intelligence" and "Counterintelligence")"Accessed From: https://www.cia.gov/library/center-for-the-study-of-intelligence/csi-publications/csi-studies/studies/vol46no2/article08.html

[80] "Report Reveals Red War Plans" Reno Evening Gazette May 24, 1951 page 14.

[81] Stiller, Werner. Beyond the Wall (Brassey's (US), 1992) page 138.

[82] "West Germany Probes Reports of East German Terror Squads" United Press International January 2, 1990 and Wenzel, Dr. Otto. "East German Plans for the Conquest and Occupation of West Berlin" Armor November-December 1994 pg. 5

[83] "Details Revealed on German 'Fifth Column'" Washington Times September 2, 1991

[84] Sleeper, Raymond S. A Lexicon of Marxist Leninist Semantics (Western Goals 1983) page 303.

the current chancellor, and other members of his Social Democrat-led coalition are absent from the list although they were politically active in the period: their credentials as left-wing critics of 'imperialist' American foreign policy apparently guaranteed their safety."[85]

Defecting Stasi officer Werner Stiller also reported that "*While officially preaching a doctrine of co-existence the GDR had in fact developed aggressive plans that included a military occupation of the FRG. Among those West Germans to be taken into 'safekeeping' were not just military personnel and politicians but also journalists, scientists, engineers, and nearly anyone entrusted with classified material.*"[86]

KGB defector Major Anatoli Golitsyn reported that the war planning strategies formulated by his former employer in the late 1950s included an estimate on how many West Germans would have to be "*isolated*" (imprisoned or killed) in order to neutralize West Germany. The KGB estimate of the number of West Germans to be executed was as high as 150,000.[87]

Reportedly, in the early stages of the Cold War, Western Europeans were terrified of a Soviet invasion and occupation of their countries. In some cases, the Western Europeans prepared themselves for what they considered an inevitable Soviet occupation of their native countries. The book <u>The Soviet Secret Police</u> noted that "*In some European countries the feeling of imminent Soviet invasion has created a psychological climate facilitating the work of INU[88]. Many people in Western Germany, for example, are studying the Russian language; their reason is, 'We'll need it when the Russians come.' Similar feelings are often in evidence in France and Switzerland.*"[89]

Meticulous plans and preparations were made for a Soviet/East German occupation of West Germany. East Germany was tasked to annex West Germany and Belgium. According to East German military plans, day one of the attack would encompass a surprise nuclear missile attack on major NATO bases in West Germany. One million Soviet, East German, and Polish troops would invade West Germany with 12,000 tanks and 25,000 troop carriers. On day 3, the defeat of West Germany was expected and thousands of East German commissars would administer occupied West Germany. On day 14, the defeat of The Netherlands, Belgium, Luxembourg, and Denmark was expected. On day 30, France was expected to fall to Warsaw Pact forces. A West German brigadier general asked his East German counterpart "*What was your unit's plan for defense?*" The East German ominously replied "*Antwerp.*"[90]

West Germany would then be administered in its entirety by the East German Army, while an occupied Berlin would be divided into several zones. These zones would be

---

[85] Michael Woodhead. "Stasi Spy Files Reveal Secret Hit Squad: High-Tech Assassination Team Operated Until Fall of Berlin Wall in 1989" <u>The Ottawa Citizen</u> May 09, 1999 page A11.
[86] Stiller, Werner. <u>Beyond the Wall</u> (Brassey's (US), 1992) page 96.
[87] Golitsyn, Anatoli. <u>The Perestroika Deception</u> (Edward Harle, 1995) Accessed From: http://www.spiritoftruth.org/The_Perestroika_Deception.pdf
[88] The INU was the Foreign Directorate of Soviet foreign intelligence.
[89] Wolin, Simon and Slusser, Robert M. <u>The Soviet Secret Police</u> (Frederick Praeger: NY 1957) pages 140-143.
[90] Wehrmacht Awards.com Accessed From: http://www.wehrmacht-awards.com/forums/showthread.php?p=1250887

administered by the East German and Soviet officials.[91] Airports and rail stations would then be managed by previously trained experts from the East. The Stasi also reprinted new maps and signs for West German cities under occupation. For example, Koenigsallee, Dusseldorf's avenue of furs, jewels and designer fashions, was to be dubbed Karl Marx Allee.[92]

According to information provided by General Sejna, Khrushchev confirmed to Soviet Marshal Rodion Malinovsky in 1963 that upon an attack on West Germany: *"I don't want to burn Europe; I want German industry intact to build socialism."*[93] The Soviets wanted to maintain elements of the hi-tech West German industrial base for the purposes of reconstruction and reparations directed to the Soviet Union. Also, the Soviets could conceivably conscript West German industries to supply the Red Army and Warsaw Pact forces with weapons for the invasions of other European countries and the United States.

Occupational currency for the conquered West Germany was first printed by the East Germans in 1980. This currency was originally Ostmark bills dated from 1955 which had the words *"Military Money"* printed over it. This special occupational currency was to be distributed to East German troops for *"operations on the territory of the adversary."* The East Germans also produced 200,000 identity cards for civilian occupational officials from East Berlin who were to govern an occupied West Germany.[94]

The NVA printed road signs (some in Flemish) for their occupation zones in the Federal Republic and points westward. Special occupation commissars were appointed from the SED. Special internment camps for foreign and domestic prisoners were also planned down to the last detail. Special shoulder boards were created for NVA field marshals. Thousands of medals were minted for NVA soldiers for the crossing of the Rhine.[95]

Other Soviet bloc troops were also tasked to fight alongside the East German and Soviet invaders of West Germany. Reportedly, the Poles would turn over authority in the occupied towns and cities of West Germany to pro-communist West German SPD cadres and the DKP. The Polish Army was delegated with the following tasks in their occupation of West Germany:
"The Surrender of Hannover according to the Polish Army's 'Bison' Exercise (April 21–28, 1971)
Due to the capitulation of the Hannover garrison, the Command of the Front has decided to provide assistance to the 5th Army by restoring the city to full function.
For this reason, for the disposition of the command of the 5th Army, we direct:
– one military police company from the NVA;
– one company for the protection of public order from the Army Security Service;

---

[91] Ingham, Robert. "Confirmed: Warsaw Pact Planned Nuclear, Chemical Onslaught on Western Europe" Agence France Presse August 3, 1991

[92] "Invasion Plans Jolt Germany: East Even Had Medals Minted for Conquest" St. Louis Post Dispatch March 29, 1993 and Fisher, Marc. "Soviets, E. Germans Had Takeover Plans: East Was Better Prepared Than Western Intelligence Knew, Documents Show" Washington Post March 17, 1993

[93] Douglass, Joseph D. "The Chemical and Biological Threat to Europe" International Security Council 1988 pages 39-40.

[94] Schonbohm, Jorg; Johnson, Peter; and Johnson, Elfi. Two Armies and One Fatherland: The End of the Nationale Volksarmee (Berghahn Books Providence RI 1996) pages 85-87.

[95] Nothnagle, Alan L. Building the East German Myth (University of Michigan Press 1999) pages 188-189.

– a group of civilian party aktiv members from the SED (20 members);
– a group of press and radio journalists from the GDR (8);
– specialists in typography and radiophony (12);
– part of a front group to secure special propaganda (24 officers, ensigns, and non-commissioned officers).

The groups mentioned above will report for the disposition of the command of the 5th Army today at 6:00 p.m. In the following days the government of the GDR will direct other groups of specialists to the city of Hannover. Each time, the arrival of these groups will be signaled.

Responsibilities of the 5th Army command include:

a) to organize the Hannover Garrison Command and appoint one of the senior officers from the 6th Armored Division as commandant of the Garrison;

b) to assign specified forces and equipment from the above-mentioned formations to the commandant of the Garrison. Simultaneously, with the support of democratic forces, to organize the regular police;

c) to organize quick and efficient press and radio information for the people;

d) to form a temporary camp for prisoners-of-war from the crew of the surrendered garrison;

e) to provide full protection and defense for depots and storehouses (both civilian and military);

f) to bring water-works, power plants, and heating plants into operation;

g) to assist the leadership that is being organized with the distribution of foodstuffs from local supplies;

h) to establish a united front municipal government recruited from activists from the KPD (German Communist Party) and the SPD (German Social Democratic Party);

i) as the removal of the ruins progresses, to bring industrial plants into production.

After a general assessment of the state of food reserves as well as the state of medical needs for civilians and prisoners, report specific requests to the staff of the Front by 11:00 a.m., April 29, 1971.

(Source: "Collection Political Administration of the Military District of Silesia, File 152448/74/42. Archives of the Ground Forces, Wroclaw.") [96]

On other occasions, defector information pointed to the fact that the Soviets would be the primary invasion force in an attack on West Germany. Defecting Czechoslovak Major General Jan Sejna noted that *"The Soviet analysts did not think the progressives would gain power without a fight with the German right-wing. They expected a conservative counter-reaction in the early 1980s-in the Third Phase of the Plan-perhaps with help from paramilitary forces and rightist sympathizers in the Bundeswehr. In this event, however, the Kremlin intended publicly to interpret such a move as a challenge to the security of Eastern Europe, and to threaten military action. Nor was this an idle threat: the Russians were indeed ready to begin a local war with Germany to support a progressive government. As early as 1968 they had allotted specific objectives for selected Soviet units to seize in a blitzkrieg operation. Ironically, there was no role in this particular exercise for the East German armed forces. The Soviet Union had no intention*

---

[96] Mastny, Vojtech and Byrne, Malcolm. A Cardboard Castle? (Central European University Press, 2005) pages. 380-381.

of encouraging anything that might lead to the unification of Germany, which was the last thing they wanted."[97]

Information reached the West from defectors and some open source information that these plans were drawn up while Stalin ruled the USSR and his European allies. Their plans for the occupation of West Berlin were extremely meticulous and thoroughly brutal in their detail and zeal in purging Germany of *"class enemies."* Upon the full defeat of NATO forces and the West Berlin police, the GDR would then immediately pursue the perceived enemies of communism. They were dubbed *"enemy forces"* by the Stasi. As early as 1985, Lt. Gen. Wolfgang Schwanitz drafted these administrative details for the new order in Berlin. The following categories of West Berliners were considered for physical extermination by the Stasi:
Politicians
Leading bureaucrats
Known economists
Scientists
Technology specialists
Military Intelligence Agents associated with the Bundeswehr
Leading anti-communist personalities and journalists.[98]

An East German attack on West Berlin was to be comprised initially of an air attack, to be followed by an artillery assault and then a troop occupation. The invading force was to be comprised of 29,000 East German and 6,000 Soviet troops. These troops were to invade West Berlin through 59 breaches in the Berlin Wall. Three hundred and thirty four tanks were to be used in the Soviet/East German invasion force. Important transportation and communications infrastructure were to be seized and the Stasi was to be given the bloody task of *"extinguishing"* the West Berlin government leadership. In 1976, a Stasi delegation visited Vietnam to learn combat tactics in enemy territories and *"the liquidation of personnel."*[99]

According to Lt. Gen. Schwanitz, *"the most significant enemy centers"* in West Berlin would be secured and occupied. A 1978 document listed 170 facilities as candidates for usage by the invading East Germans. The facilities listed in a document for the district of Kreuzberg was indicative of the thoroughness of the East German planning: police weapons depot; Customs Bureau; Customs Investigator Bureau; State Printing Shop; Telecommunications Bureau; Artisan's Chamber of Commerce; and the sewage treatment plant were to be all seized by East German forces. The twelve districts in West Berlin were to be transformed into District Administrative Centers by the occupying East Germans. Each new center would be administered by 40-47 East German officials. These centers were to be subordinated to Command Groups, each consisting of eighty appointed officials. Each Group was to be modeled after the Stasi and was responsible for various security related tasks for the occupied population. Each group would be divided into Operative Groups dealing with: counterespionage, ministerial, economic, and transportation security. The fifth Operative Group would specialize in combating *"political ideological diversions"* and *"underground activities."* They would be tasked with the

---

[97] Sejna, Jan. We Will Bury You (Sidgwick & Jackson; First edition 1982) Accessed From: http://www.spiritoftruth.org/We_Will_Bury_You.pdf
[98] Boll, Michael M. "By Blood, Not Ballots: German Unification Communist Style" Parameters Spring 1994 pages 70-71.
[99] "East Germans Planned to Conquer West Berlin: Historian" Agence France Presse September 14, 2000

suppression of resistance to the communist occupation forces and their collaborators. The Berlin Wall would still exist and would only be dismantled when all resistance in West Berlin was exterminated by security forces. Once total victory was achieved, then divided Berlin would be united under East German governance. As early as 1980, the East Germans also printed 4.9 billion worth of occupation Ostmarks for issuance in the economy of occupied West Berlin. In 1985, special military medals for bravery were minted by the National People's Army (NVA) to be awarded to the city's *"liberators."* They were stored in a special *"medals cellar."*

Based on the East German occupation plans for West Berlin, Boll also suspected that equally meticulous war plans also existed for West Germany. He also believed that the federated character of West Germany's provinces would be maintained by the East German occupiers. Boll speculated that one or more *"supra German"* provinces would emerge in a defeated and occupied West Germany.[100]

Berlin's city government would be overthrown and the Stasi would be tasked in purging political and other *"class enemies."* These enemies would include anti-communists, businessmen, anti-leftists, civil servants, and police officials. The Stasi drew up such lists of specific individuals who were then to be dispatched to *"internment camps."* The invasion of West Berlin would be known as Day X and would involve the Stasi and East German Army troops storming through 59 breaches in the Berlin Wall. All means of communications and transportation in Berlin would be captured and churches shut down. Economic assets and the means of communication would be harnessed by the occupying East German forces. Berlin would be administered by 12 neighborhood administrative offices, according to a document drawn up for the head of the Stasi Erich Mielke. The document itself was drawn up by the District Leader of the Berlin Area of the Ministry of State Security, Lieutenant-General Wolfgang Schwanitz. This plan for the occupation of West Berlin was in force as late as 1985, according to historian Dr. Otto Wenzel.[101]

During the period of *"glasnost"* and *"perestroika,"* the East Germans commenced various military exchanges with the West German Bundeswehr in an effort to combat the perception of East Berlin as a mortal enemy of the West. For example, in April 1989, a two day defense studies seminar between military scientists and high-ranking officers of the Bundeswehr and East German NVA took place in Hamburg at the Institute for Peace Research and Security Policy, which was directed by pro-Soviet SPD official Egon Bahr.[102]

Also, despite the allegedly reduced tensions of the between NATO and the Warsaw Pact in the Gorbachev era, Moscow and its allies continued its war planning and exercises against Bonn. In April 1989, 18,500 troops of the Soviet Union and East Germany conducted exercises in Cottbus.[103] In 1988-1989, formerly top secret documents outlined the advanced course for the senior officer corps of the East German Army in which the *"instructions of the Commander-in-Chief of the Pact's Joint Armed Forces regarding the operational mission of troops and naval forces"* laid out that: *"The goal of the operation is to liberate the territories of the GDR and CSSR, to occupy the economically important regions of the FRG east of the Rhine, and to create*

---

[100] Boll, Michael M. "By Blood, Not Ballots: German Unification Communist Style" <u>Parameters</u> Spring 1994 pages 70-72.

[101] Wenzel, Dr. Otto. "East German Plans for the Conquest and Occupation of West Berlin" <u>Armor</u> November-December 1994 pages 5 and 9-10.

[102] "NVA-Bundeswehr Meeting in Hamburg" <u>East German News Agency</u> April 3, 1989

[103] "GDR-Soviet Military Exercises in Cottbus Area" <u>East German News Agency</u> April 27, 1989

the right circumstances for a transition to a general offensive aimed at bringing about the withdrawal of the European NATO states from the war." The exercise *"Staff Training 89"* called for the utilization of 76 nuclear weapons, some of which having a high yield in the West German provinces of Schleswig-Holstein. Another purpose of this usage of mass destruction weapons was also to induce panic and disorder in the Western democracies. This would thus have the effect of weakening the resistance of the Free World and the cohesion of the NATO allies. As one document stated: *"It is desirable to consider (...) nuclear attacks on such centers as Hannover or Brunswick, Kiel and Bremen. The destruction of these cities will likely cause a complete disorganization of political life, the economy, etc. It will significantly influence the creation of panic in areas of nuclear strikes. The exploitation of the effects of strikes by our propaganda may contribute to the spread of panic among enemy armies and populations (...). In order to exclude Denmark from the war as quickly as possible, nuclear strikes should be launched at Esbjerg (an important strategic point in the NATO system) and Roskilde (Zealand Island), and subsequently a widespread special propaganda action aimed at deepening the existing panic should be conducted to warn Denmark's troops and civilian population of the consequences of further resistance and the threat that, in the event of continuation of the war, further atomic strikes will occur."*[104]

Even under the *"reformist"* communist governments in East Berlin, the Soviet and East German armies carried out military exercises aimed at the invasion and occupation of West Germany. The Agence France Presse reported in 1991 that *"as late as June 1990, eight months after the fall of the Berlin Wall, the NVA's (Nationale Volksarmee/National People's Army of East Germany) 5th Army carried out joint exercises with the Soviet military that still rehearsed for a westward offensive in northern Germany. The plan involved the use of chemical weapons and up to 87 nuclear warheads. And a similar war game involving Soviet and East German generals was planned for September, less than a month before German unification."*[105] In February 1990, 400 National People's Army and 15,900 Soviet troops engaged in an exercise in East Germany.[106] In March 1990, a tactical air defense force training exercise took place with the armed forces of East Germany, Soviet Union, Czechoslovakia, and Poland participating.[107] This exercise also involved the armies of East Germany, Czechoslovakia, Poland, and the Western Group of Soviet Forces.[108]

In August 1990, 15,000 troops of the Group of Soviet Forces in Germany conducted exercises in the Beelitz, Potsdam, and Cottbus Districts.[109] In August 1990, it was reported that the East German Army was to begin a maneuver code named *Nordwind* the thrust of which was

---

[104] "Warsaw Pact Military Planning in Central Europe: Revelations From the East German Archives" Cold War International History Project Bulletin Woodrow Wilson International Center for Scholars, Washington, D.C. Fall 1992 pg. 14 Accessed http://wilsoncenter.org/topics/pubs/ACF1C1.pdf
[105] Piotrowski, Pawel. "A Landing Operation in Denmark: The Polish Military's Losses in the First Phase of a Warsaw Pact Offensive Were to Reach 50 Percent" Wprost (Warsaw), no. 25, 23 June 2002 Accessed from http://www.dupi.dk/webdocs/landing_eng.pdf
[106] "Soviet Troops Begin Military Exercise in GDR" Xinhua February 5, 1990
[107] "Warsaw Treaty Air Defence Exercise" BBC Summary of World Broadcasts March 26, 1990
[108] Ibid.
[109] "Soviet Armed Forces to Hold Military Exercises in GDR" Xinhua August 8, 1990

aimed at the Federal Republic. It involved 300 troops and 15 tanks.[110] In July 1990, it was reported that the Soviet Army would keep 600 tactical nuclear weapons in East Germany, even for years after the divided country reunified.[111] Such an arrangement would continue the reality of having the Soviet nuclear dagger pointed at Europe from the heart of West Germany, despite reunification. Certainly, if Moscow gained a neutral, socialist, and reunified Germany as an ally, Bonn could possibly show an open-mind to such a Soviet move.

In late 1989 and 1990, the SED sought to further solidify their economic power in the East in preparation for taking full control of a reunified Germany, even under the governance of a conservative CDU-CSU government. Since the SED believed that money commanded tremendous political power in capitalist societies, they decided to aggregate as much hard currency and property in Eastern Germany as their existing assets and financial schemes would permit. This peaceful reunification would bloodlessly accomplish what decades of military planning could not achieve. In November 1989, the Stasi and SED tasked a core group of agents to infiltrate East German state-owned companies in anticipation of and preparation for the Party's return to power after re-unification. From November 1989 to January 1990, the initial phase of the plan known as *"Operation Shredder."* Agents destroyed incriminating documents linking the secret team to either the SED or the Stasi. The secret Stasi team infiltrated citizens' groups and the East German parliamentary committee charged with disbanding the secret police. The secret team was ordered to secure former Communist holdings in Germany and abroad to create *"a new empire, initially based on economic power."* Once the industrial economic powerhouse of the Stasi and SED was in place, it was supposed to fund the neo-Communist Party for Democratic Socialism. In the second phase of the operation, from January to March 1990, the Stasi was to be transformed from a *"mechanism for vulgar repression to a qualified economic and administrative organization."* In a third phase, from April to September 1990, underground agents were to work their way into leading positions at a number of the 8,000 state-owned East German companies.[112]

Reportedly, such efforts that were undertaken by the SED seemed to pay off in the initial stages of German reunification. In late October 1990, the Minister for Special Tasks for Chancellor Kohl Guenther Krauss, called for the government to break up *"networks of communists."* Krauss noted to the Bonn newspaper General Amzeiger, *"There are many networks at different levels: of union officials, party functionaries, industrial managers, in public service, in the government labor and finance offices."* Workers in eastern Germany complained that their current factory bosses even under the regime of *"privatization"* were the same old SED bosses. The Bonn Rundschau newspaper reported that the vast majority 2,000 officials in the *Treuhandanstalt* (the agency charged with privatizing state-owned enterprises in eastern Germany) were former SED officials.[113]

---

[110] "Denial of Welt am Sonntag Claim of Major NVA Exercise" East German News Agency August 21, 1990

[111] Gertz, Bill. "Soviet Nuclear Arms Will Stay in Germany" Washington Times July 31, 1990 page A5.

[112] "Bold German Economic Plot Reported: Communists Allegedly Ordered Stasi Police to Infiltrate State Firms" The San Francisco Chronicle November 24, 1990

[113] Fleming, Joseph. "E. German Loyalists Keep Important Posts" Washington Times October 25, 1990 page A9.

After the *"fall"* of the Soviet Union in December 1991, the new Russian leadership did not halt their program to influence the reunified Germany. Moscow used the tools of espionage and economic domination to draw the reunified German Federal Republic into its orbit. German counterintelligence found that Russian operations within the Federal Republic were on the increase by mid-1992, thanks to the Stasi networks that survived the collapse of the East German government. Chief Prosecutor Alexander von Stahl noted that Russian espionage was in the process of *"widening"* its German network and *"reactivating"* an estimated 400 former East German Stasi officers and agents. The SVR is also reported to have recruited *"a large number"* of past members of the former East German Main Intelligence Directorate (HVA). Many of the increased espionage activities were staged from Russian military installations in the eastern Germany. These installations were linked to Russia by Ministry of Security/Federal Counterintelligence Service-administered troop trains which were not subjected to inspections by German authorities. Von Stahl noted that there was *"no noticeable change"* in intelligence gathering from former Soviet military bases, such as the headquarters of the Western Group of the Commonwealth of Independent States (CIS) Joint Armed Forces in Wunsdorf outside Berlin.[114] After the reunification of the two Germanys in October 1990, some Stasi and HVA officers profited from trade with the remaining communist nations. One notorious example was the case of the former Stasi General and high ranking East German SED foreign trade official Alexander Schalck-Golodkowski. He opened a business in the re-unified Germany. Golodkowski also owned a German firm that specialized in trade with Red China, thus transferring his money-making acumen to a different communist master.[115]

Under the Chancellorships of Gerhard Schroeder (SPD) and Angela Merkel (CDU-CSU), Moscow achieved a large degree of political and economic hegemony over Germany. Such measures fit into the original Soviet plans to achieve a reunified and neutralized government in Berlin which would lean in Moscow's direction. Over 40% of the imported natural gas originated from Russia. Hence, German industries and homes were heavily dependent on this Russian natural gas. In November 2010, Russian ruler Vladimir Putin mocked Germany's dependence on Russia gas, quipping to assembled businessmen *"how will you heat your houses?...Even for firewood, you'd have to go to Siberia."* The SPD also accepted Germany's energy dependence on Russia in the fear of antagonizing their powerful Eastern neighbor. Veteran SPD politician Hans-Ulrich Klose noted that mutual trade and dependency between Russia and Germany would limit the chance that Moscow would *"to sneak out and do something crazy."* Former SPD leader and Chancellor Gerhard Schroeder also headed the Gazprom-controlled consortium that oversaw the construction of a new natural gas pipeline between Russia and Germany. The CEO of the state-owned Russian Gazprom company Aleksei Miller remarked that this pipeline represented a *"fundamentally new phase in cooperation between Russia and Germany."* Former officials of the SED, such as the former Deputy Chief of the East German oil and gas industry, became officials at the Berlin headquarters of Gazprom. Former Stasi agents were also employed by Gazprom in Germany. Stasi alumni held positions as the

---

[114] Waller, J. Michael. <u>Secret Empire: The KGB in Russia Today</u> (Westview Press, 1994) pages 142-144.

[115] "It's Alexander the freight; Life of East German wheeler-dealer" <u>The Birmingham Post</u> April 29, 2000 Accessed From:
http://www.thefreelibrary.com/It's+Alexander+the+freight%3B+Life+of+East+German+wheeler-dealer.-a061851889

directors of personnel and finance of Gazprom Germania. The director of the Nord Stream pipeline consortium was Matthia Warnig, a decorated Stasi officer. Gazprom cooperated with powerful German firms, such as EON and BASF.[116]

It is this author's belief four main sets of collaborators would emerge in a West Berlin and West Germany defeated by an invasion of the Soviet Union and East Germany. They would include the following categories:
1) Pro-Soviet and/or pro-Soviet SPD (Social Democratic) activists and parliamentarians.
2) DKP (West German Communist Party) and SEW (Socialist Unity Party of West Berlin) activists and officials.
3) A small minority of greedy, pro-détente-minded, or even secretly Marxist industrialists and CSU/CDU parliamentarians who strongly believed in political and economic engagement with the slave masters of the East.
4) Pro-Soviet elements of the West German neo-Nazi movement.

Clearly, pro-Soviet leftists in the SPD and the outright communists in the DKP probably would have provided the bulk of collaborators with the Soviet and Warsaw Pact occupiers in West Germany. Ideological statements and previous political actions by individuals in this category would lend credence to this claim. Data from the public domain, Bloc defectors, and declassified transcripts are currently available and back up this admittedly controversial assertion.

Early on, the SED realized the important role West German progressive leftists would play in the reunification with East Germany. The early East German leaders did place some hope in the West German Left overthrowing the CDU-CSU government in Bonn. SED Chairman Walter Ulbricht was quoted in Pravda in December 1961 as stating that *"The prerequisite for reuniting Germany is the overthrow of the reactionary regime in West Germany by the progressive forces in West Germany itself."*[117]

Defecting Czechoslovak Major General Jan Sejna noted that *"...the Kremlin ordered the Warsaw Pact countries to co-ordinate their policies towards the SDP (Social Democrats in West Germany) to make it seem that we were responding to SDP initiatives and thus enhance the prestige of that party. But we had to take care lest the SDP be branded as pro-Communist, and so we would make periodical attacks on it. Meanwhile, we Czechs and the East Germans channeled funds to sustain its left-wing faction."*[118]

When former high-level Soviet official Igor Glagolev attended a conference on the economic problems of disarmament in Kiel, West Germany in 1961, he met with SPD Bundestag member F. Baade. Baade represented the interests of the shipbuilding workers' trade unions in Kiel. Members of this union were involved in constructing ships for export to the USSR. Glagolev noted that the SPD sought to impose a *"plan"* in order to organize the world economy according to the precepts of socialism. Baade briefed Glagolev on the activities of the pro-Soviet

---

[116] Feifer, Gregory. "Too Special A Friendship: Is Germany Questioning Russia's Embrace?" RFERL News July 11, 2011 Accessed From: http://www.rferl.org/content/germany_and_russia_too_special_a_relationship/24262486.html

[117] Sleeper, Raymond S. A Lexicon of Marxist Leninist Semantics (Western Goals 1983) page 122.

[118] Sejna, Jan. We Will Bury You (Sidgwick & Jackson; First edition 1982) Accessed From: http://www.spiritoftruth.org/We_Will_Bury_You.pdf

core of the West German SPD and its faction in the Bundestag. Baade himself belonged to this faction and maintained extensive connections with the USSR.[119]

The East Germans and Soviets also dispatched agents to West Germany who posed as anti-communists seeking freedom in the West. Such refugees were tasked with the assignment to climb the ladders within West German society and achieve political influence. Such political influence could then be used to promote policies beneficial to Moscow and East Berlin. One infamous case centered on Gunther Guillaume. Guillaume was sent to West Germany as illegal agent from East Germany and was instructed by his superiors to flee East Germany and serve the cause of democracy and penetrate the SPD. He became a chief adviser to Willi Brandt, who accepted Soviet war gains, played down the USSR threat, and accepted the sovereignty of East Germany in a treaty signed with Moscow in August 1970.[120]

Egon Bahr was another prominent SPD official who supported further openings to the communist world under the rubric of peace and détente. Former Romanian DIE (Department of External Information) General Ion Pacepa reported that Bahr had drawn up a secret plan to withdraw West Germany from NATO in exchange for a Soviet guarantee of non-aggression. He allegedly advocated the plan as a means towards re-unifying Germany, and thus creating a supposedly neutral, socialist Federal Republic.[121] Bahr was an example of a hardcore ideological sympathizer with dictatorial communism who was also a very prominent member of the West German political establishment. He was also known to display an utterly brutal contempt towards the anti-communist community in West Germany. Had the East Germans occupied the West, Bahr would have served East Berlin in purging anti-communists. Hermann von Berg, formerly a negotiator for the East German government, recalled a meeting with Bahr in the early 1970s. Regarding critical West German journalists, Bahr noted to Berg that *"If this would be Chicago I would order a gang to kill them."* Berg brought Bahr's brutal mentality up to East German Prime Minister Willi Stoph, who retorted *"At least Bahr belongs to those who have a feeling for power. But you should know that the left-wing Social Democrats and we come from the same tradition."*[122]

Another West German SPD official named Karsten Voigt was a prolific visitor to the Central Committee of the SED. Formerly classified documents of the SED pointed to the fact that Voigt was a staunch collaborator and admirer of the East German Communist government. One secret SED document noted that *"Repeatedly Karsten D. Voigt spoke positively about the policy of the SED. Its big merit is its programmatic clarity, its knowledge about the problems, its strength of political organization, and its unity."* Karsten noted that *"many things the communists in the GDR achieved politically and organisationally are well done and are, like, e.g., the training system, exemplary also for his (Voigt's) party."* Another SED document reported this disturbing piece of information: *"Serious is the accusation that Voigt gave pieces of advice to the SED how it could proceed most cleverly against civil rights campaigners in order to avoid public stir. At any rate, in the files one finds a 'note about confidential information by K.D. Voigt' of July 8, 1988. According to that the foreign affairs specialist of the SPD has*

---

[119] Glagolev, Dr. Igor S. Post-Andropov Kremlin Strategy (Association for Cooperation of Democratic Countries, 1984) page 43.
[120] Pincher, Chapman. The Secret Offensive (Sidgwick & Jackson 1986) pages 164-165.
[121] "Five Alleged Bonn Spies Cleared" Stars and Stripes September 28, 1978 page 23.
[122] Nasselstein, Peter. "Political Irrationalism From An Orgonomic Point of View" May 2, 2007 Accessed From: http://www.orgonomie.net/hdoeng07.htm

pointed out to the Central Committee officials Manfred Uschner and Karl-Heinz Wagner that the civil rights campaigners Barbel Bohley and Wolfgang Templin, who had left East Germany with a limited exit permit, wanted to test on August 6th the re-entry promise of the GDR leadership. Voigt added according to the file note: 'In his (Voigt's) personal opinion it would be the best solution to let them enter East Germany for the time being to arrest and deport them in the wake of illegal activities. They (the dissidents) and the secret services behind them reckon with and hope for that the security services of the GDR would hinder their entry into the country. This one intends to play off against the international security cooperation of SED and SPD. '"[123]

The East German leadership clearly viewed the West German political classes as elements to be penetrated and manipulated to the advantage of Moscow and East Berlin. A divided West German society would have serve as a weakened enemy ripe for takeover by either extreme leftist elements or a direct Warsaw Pact invasion. Stasi officer Vogel noted to his former subordinate Werner Stiller that *"For the last six years the West German government has been headed by a liberal-social democratic coalition. From our point of view, there are good reasons to feel satisfied with the results of that period.* **_Particularly through the policy of détente we have been able to end the FRG's claim to sole legitimacy and gain worldwide diplomatic recognition for the GDR. Admittedly détente has caused an ideological slackness in certain groups at home as well as a rise in emigration applications but on the whole the class struggle has continued to advance in our direction_**…*I wonder whether you have given any thought to next year's general election in the FRG. Even though we prefer that the present coalition remain in office there is no certainty of that happening. We must therefore be prepared for the advent of a right wing government. That means taking off the kid gloves and doing everything possible to make life difficult for the conservatives. Our colleagues in political intelligence have already established some effective positions in conservative ranks without diminishing their presence in the two coalition parties…For some time now we've observed a sizable growth in the anti-nuclear movement. Because its opposition to the policies of the Bonn government benefits us in the long run, we've given the movement a modest degree of support. At the moment, however, its attacks on the liberal-social democratic coalition make us less than enthusiastic. Of course with a conservative government in power these environmental nuts could be unleashed to destabilize the entire system. The question is how best to help them…But with a new government we can mobilize our heaviest artillery.* **_The time is rapidly approaching when the simple procurement of scientific or even political information will not suffice. We must find active ways to weaken the West not through a full scale attack but by slow and systematic capture of individual positions. Just consider how much Western influence is declining in country after country in the so-called developing world. The present day class struggle demands that economics, politics, diplomacy, and intelligence form a cohesive whole._** *Think about that a while and work out some new ideas. When fewer tactical considerations need to be shown toward the FRG I don't want to be caught empty handed."*

Werner Stiller wrote *"Despite my own deep estrangement from the GDR my greatest anger was directed at those gullible Western politicians who accepted the concepts of détente and peaceful co-existence at face value. From my unique vantage point, the communist strategy was unmistakenly clear-breaking the barriers of resistance to acquire Western technology and then continuing its own massive arms buildup and expansion of power."*[124]

---

[123] Ibid.
[124] Stiller, Werner. <u>Beyond the Wall</u> (Brassey's (US), 1992) pages 142-143.

The East Germans also viewed the noisy and militant West German leftist youth as an opportunity to further divide the population from the government in Bonn. An East German teacher reportedly told his class that the rebellious West German youth *"are dissatisfied with capitalist society and favor the establishment of democratic relationships, although they have not yet properly understood that the future belongs to communism."* The West German Socialist German Student Union (SDS) praised East Germany for its alleged advances in education and other fields.[125]

In August 1965, two West German leftist student representatives Wolfgang Lefevre and Peter Damerow signed an East German SED-initiated petition that called for peace in Vietnam. The East Germans also offered their support for a West German SDS plan to blockade the Autobahn which led to West Berlin from East German territory. In late 1967, the West German SDS President Karl-Dietrich Wolff told an East German source that the anti-US military base campaign was supported by the West German labor unions. Furthermore, he also admitted that the West German SDS was able to smuggle 150 American soldiers per month out of the country. In February 1967, a conference in solidarity with Vietnam was held in West Berlin and was attended by American radical leftists such as H. Rap Brown, Stokley Carmichael, representatives of socialist-communist states, the East German SED official youth group (the FDJ), pro-Chinese West German groups, and the West German SDS.[126]

The cooperation of the West German SDS with the official SED youth organization (FDJ) was seen as an *"act of defiance against the anti-communist ideology of the Federal Republic and an attempt to weaken the hard and fast categories of the Cold War bloc system."* The West German SDS demanded diplomatic recognition of East Germany. The CIA noted in a report that the *"SED apparently hopes to establish a network of intermediate-level control in student organizations, and then to use these contacts to manipulate the organizations."*[127] By 1968, West German New Leftists maintained ties to PLO terrorists, Czech, and Cuban agents.[128]

The East German SED leadership clearly saw the fruits of leftwing subversion amongst the students in West Germany and the increasingly open borders travel policy between East and West Germany. A 1967 document of the SED Department of International Relations noted that *"Discord is developing between the classes in West Germany, although slowly. Representatives of both the reactionary monopoly capital and the Social Democratic Party's leadership are currently included in the Bonn government. Students play a major role in West Germany in the opposition against the government…It is becoming more and more difficult for the imperialists to spread their lies about the GDR…Two million West Germans come to the GDR every year, and 1 million travel to West Germany. You can draw your own conclusions about developments in the two German states."*[129]

---

[125] Resurgence Volumes 1-2 1966 page 109.

[126] Klimke, Martin. The Other Alliance (Princeton University Press 2011) pages 62, 84, 179, 172-173.

[127] Brown, Timothy Scott. West Germany and the Global Sixties (Cambridge University Press 2013) pages 42-43.

[128] McDonald, Congressman Larry P. "Terrorism in West Germany" Congressional Record September 14, 1979 pages 24746-24747.

[129] Memorandum on a meeting with a delegation from the Supreme People's Assembly of the DPRK on 3 July 1967 3 July 1967 Department of International Relations Berlin, 18 July 1967 Accessed From:

Out of a core of the West German New Left political scene, the Baader-Meinhof Gang (later the Red Army Faction) was born. A founder of the Baader-Meinhof Gang, Ulrike Meinhof, condemned elements of the Western European Left for criticizing the Soviet invasion of Czechoslovakia. Meinhof wrote in the September 1968 issue of Konkret: *"On August 21 the European Left gave up its solidarity, its sympathy, its gratitude towards the Soviet Union as the first Socialist country as that state which defeated German fascism at Stalingrad."*[130]

The nucleus of the Baader-Meinhof Gang leadership had longstanding ties to the Communists in East Berlin. A Baader-Meinhof Gang leader Klaus Rainer Rohl admitted in the 1974 book Fuenf Finger sind keine Faust (Five Fingers Do Not Make a Fist), that he was a member of the illegal West German Kommunistische Partei Deutschlands (KPD-Communist Party of Germany) until 1964. Rohl also admitted to receiving money from the KPD to fund his leftist periodical Konkret. Meanwhile, the Free University in Berlin (FU) was infiltrated by communists from East Germany and students from West Germany who wanted to escape the compulsory military service. The FU was a hotbed of New Left activities. The book International Terrorism in the Contemporary World revealed that *"specialists from the German Democratic Republic also aided this development by originating the so-called STAMOKAP theory, which refers to government monopolistic capitalism, which must be overcome. Leftist organizations in the Federal Republic of Germany readily adopted this theory, although no one was certain that it had been imported from the German Democratic Republic."*[131]

Early on, the Baader-Meinhof Gang forged covert ties with the East Germans and Palestinian Arab terrorists. In 1970, Baader Meinhof terrorists flew out of East Berlin to points in the Middle East on false passports.[132] In 1970, the first safe house in East Berlin was set up for the Baader-Meinhof Gang. The East Germans also supplied the Baader-Meinhof Gang with false passports, money, paramilitary training, and protected entry/exit from East Germany.[133] Between 1970 and 1972, Baader-Meinhof Gang terrorists traveled to East Berlin and flew from Berlin-Schoenefeld International Airport on the East German airline Interflug to Lebanon. In Lebanon, the Baader-Meinhof Gang terrorists were trained in PLO camps in marksmanship and the use of explosives.[134]

Clearly, the Baader-Meinhof Gang terrorists sought the overthrow of the Bonn government and its replacement with a radical Marxist dictatorship. In early 1975, the imprisoned leaders of the Baader-Meinhof Gang were interviewed by Der Spiegel. Baader-Meinhof Gang leaders called West Germany *"An imperialistic center. US colony. US military base. Leading imperialistic power in West Europe, in the EG (European Community). Second*

---

http://digitalarchive.wilsoncenter.org/document/112306.pdf?v=4efbcb7e75a6896768003df6659456c0

[130] Goren, Roberta. The Soviet Union and Terrorism (Allen & Unwin 1984) pages 160-174.

[131] Livingston, Marius H.; Kress, Lee Bruce; Wanek, Marie G. International Terrorism in the Contemporary World (Greenwood Press 1978) pages 199-200.

[132] Goren, Roberta. The Soviet Union and Terrorism (Allen & Unwin 1984) pages 160-174.

[133] Sterling, Claire. The Terror Network (Penguin Group (USA) Incorporated 1983) pages 270-271.

[134] Livingston, Marius H.; Kress, Lee Bruce; Wanek, Marie G. International Terrorism in the Contemporary World (Greenwood Press 1978) pages 196-197.

strongest military power in NATO. Representative of the US imperialistic interests in Western Europe." All of the Baader-Meinhof Gang leaders admitted that they were *"Marxists."*[135]

The Baader-Meinhof Gang also seemed to endorse militant anti-Jewish prejudices. They even agreed that Nazi anti-Semitism was just a facet of revolutionary anti-capitalism and therefore deserved support. Ulrike Meinhof of the Baader-Meinhof Gang noted that *"Auschwitz means that 6 million Jews were killed, and thrown onto the waste heap of Europe, for what they were: money-Jews. Finance capital and the banks, the hard core of the system of imperialism and capitalism, had turned the hatred of men against money and exploitation, and against the Jews... Antisemitism is really a hatred of capitalism."*[136]

After the arrests of the Baader-Meinhof Gang leadership, the remaining terrorists and other leftists reformulated themselves by the late 1970s as the Red Army Faction (RAF). East German ruler Erich Honecker supported the RAF as a means of *"self-defense against the repressive policies of the capitalist West."*[137] Hence, it was more than possible that the RAF would have been activated by the East Germans as a sabotage force in the event of an invasion of West Germany by Warsaw Pact forces. Perhaps the leadership and fighters of the RAF would have become officers in the army and police forces of a newly, reunified communist Germany.

The East Germans and Soviets controlled the West German KPD (after 1968, the DKP) as a means of creating a dedicated cadre and a force of potential collaborators in the event of an invasion and occupation of West Germany. After 1946, the KPD expanded its already existing Inter-Zonal contacts and took orders from the SED Headquarters in the Soviet Sector of Berlin. A number of prominent communists resigned their posts in after October 1946 and reappeared as leaders of trade unions in the Western Zones of Germany. This action pointed to a massive case of KPD infiltration of the Western German trade unions. The SED also provided the KPD with financial support before and after the 1948 currency reform in the Western Zones of Germany. Documents available at the time such as the *"M Plan"* of 1947 highlighted the Inter-Zonal connections between the SED and KPD.[138]

The Berlin Central Committee's Cadre Department operated a *"Western Germany Desk"* beginning in 1945. KPD officials were responsible for activities within the French, British, and American Zones of Germany, which then became the Zones Leadership and then the West Commission. KPD Zonal officials in the West reported to Marshal Zhukov and Walter Ulbricht. Since the SPD-KPD merger of 1946, the KPD were also controlled by the East Berlin-based leadership of the SED in the Soviet Zone of Germany. The Soviet Zone authorities also provided printed matter and newsprint to the KPD in the West. Ex-Nazis also provided protection payments to the KPD in exchange for a good word in the de-Nazification trials. Since 1946, SED functionaries who were apprehended by Western authorities were discovered to have large sums of Reichsmarks in their possession. These Reichsmarks were then disbursed by the SED's Sonderkonto West to local communists. After the 1948 currency reform in the West, the SED raised money through black market sales as a means of funding the KPD in the West. The Soviet Military Administration (SMAD) also paid hard currency Deutsche Marks (DM) to the KPD in

---

[135] Ibid, pages 196-197.

[136] Bogdanor, Paul. "The Communists As They Really Are" Accessed From: http://www.paulbogdanor.com/left/communists.html

[137] Schweizer, Peter. Reagan's War (Random House LLC 2003) page 259.

[138] Nettl, J.P. The Eastern Zone and Soviet Policy in Germany 1945-50 (Oxford University Press, 1951) pages 260-261.

the West. The West Commission of the SED was formed in February 1949. It enjoyed support from Stalin and the Main Department of Information, the Ministry of Foreign Affairs, and the Ministry of Foreign Trade. By 1952, it employed 300-400 workers with six departments including an Operative Group. Top SED officials from the East traveled undercover to West Germany to control and guide KPD meetings. Western departments were also created for all East German mass organizations such as the state-run FDGB's Bureau of Trade Union Unity.[139]

The Dreizonenvorstand (DZV), the headquarters of the Western Communist Party (KPD) was controlled by the SED Central Secretariat in Berlin as of 1949 (and before). Its members and leaders traveled and conferred with the SED Politburo and the Soviet Military Administration on matters of policy and to receive orders. The old time communist named Richard Stahlmann was the SED's liaison with the KPD. The KPD maintained 350,000 members. Many West Germans were reportedly fearful of a Soviet occupation of the Western Zone and therefore did not openly antagonize the KPD. Sources of income for the KPD included the sale of various commodities smuggled from the Soviet Zone and donations from individuals who wanted to avoid reprisals in the event of a Soviet occupation of the Western Zones of Germany.[140]

German Communists urged their cadres at a congress in 1950 to launch sabotage in a so-called *"fighting program."* The subversive plan included: incitement of strikes at ports and heavy industries; discouragement of recruiting for the West German Federal Police forces; convert to communism former Wehrmacht officers; mass demonstrations in cities; and inducement of West German Ruhr industrialists to invest in the GDR.[141]

Stalin and President Wilhelm Pieck of the SED conversed in April 1952 on *"how should the party continue its struggle in West Germany in the future."* Cooperation with neo-Nazi and nationalist elements in West Germany was also supported by the Soviets and the SED as a means of creating a united front of anti-Western forces. It was noted at the conversation that *"The main task at the present time is to achieve unity of the working class. The CC SED has recently sent a letter to the SPD CC with proposals on the issues of German unity and the peace treaty. However, it is most likely that the right-wing leadership of the Social Democrats will reject this proposal as well. Our next task is to pool all bourgeois nationalist forces together. In the nearest future, we will hold the 'Conference of the Thousand' with participation of various patriotic groups…The conference will elect a permanent presidium for organization of coordinated actions in the struggle for unity and the peace treaty. This will help us to expand the movement. The decisive issue will be the strengthening of the Communist Party of (West) Germany (KPD). In the last year, it achieved good results in its struggle against remilitarization and for the German unity. In this connection, there is a danger that the Adenauer government might ban the Communist Party…The SED CC tried to help the KPD by sending instructors and authorized officials to West Germany from the GDR."*

Pieck also called for the prevention of a General Treaty by *"strikes, 'appeal for peace,' collecting signatures of the population in West and East Germany, drafting of a national*

---

[139] Major, Patrick. The Death of the KPD (Oxford University Press 1998) pages 60-73.
[140] Central Intelligence Agency "Soviet Control Mechanism in Germany" May 26, 1949 Accessed From:
http://www.foia.cia.gov/sites/default/files/document_conversions/89801/DOC_0000258562.pdf
[141] "German Reds Urge Sabotage in West" New York Times August 27, 1950 page 20.

program on behalf of the Presidium of the 'Conference of the Thousand.' The government of the GDR will make a statement to the effect that it does not recognize the General Treaty."[142]

Even in the early days of the Khrushchev era in the USSR, Moscow ordered its agents and diplomats to support the pro-Soviet elements of the SPD and West German industrialists. In December 1955, Valerian Zorin, the first Soviet Ambassador to West Germany (Federal Republic or FRG), received instructions *"to give necessary attention and support to the Social Democratic party and those bourgeois circles that stood in opposition to the policy of the Adenauer government."*[143]

The SED maintained an indoctrination center in Bautzen Saxony targeted for defectors from West Germany, the United States, and other non-communist countries. Twenty American civilians and soldiers were reportedly some of the students enrolled at this center. They were brainwashed to hate the West and their movements were controlled by the Volkspolizei (People's Police). The Western defectors are provided with ration coupons and Ostmarks (East German currency) for use in state-owned stores and access to the foreigners club at a former mansion. Western and American defectors were also billeted rent free in the Hotel Stadt Bautzen.[144]

Occasional deserters from the East German Army defected to the West and after finding life difficult or less than glamorous, moved back to the East. Such re-defections served as excellent propaganda for the image of East Germany and dissuaded other would be defectors from East Germany from ever going over to the West.[145] Such defectors served to erode the image of West Germany in the eyes of its population and world opinion.

As of 1956, two special demoralization committees were set up in East Germany to undermine NATO. One committee was charged with propagandizing anti-colonialism amongst French troops of North African descent stationed in West Germany and was headed by the German Communist named Albert Schreiner. Another committee headed by ex-Wehrmacht generals tried to win over former Wehrmacht generals in the Bundeswehr to undermine the credibility of the West German government.[146]

The so-called peace movement served to cripple the defense position of the West German armed forces and NATO forces stationed there. This would serve to pave the way for the Soviets and the rest of the Warsaw Pact to intimidate, gain hegemony over, and even conquer West Germany. Erich Honecker noted in 1985 that *"Our aim is to isolate the most aggressive forces of imperialism, provide encouragement to the realistic circles in the capitalist states and to achieve the revival of détente…The peace movement is proving to be an effective force for counteracting*

---

[142] "Conversations between Joseph V. Stalin and SED leadership" April 1, 1952 Cold War International History Project Accessed From: http://www.wilsoncenter.org/index.cfm?topic_id=1409&fuseaction=va2.document&identifier=5034FD88-96B6-175C-93105576DC034850&sort=Collection&item=Stalin%20and%20the%20Cold%20War

[143] Patrick M. Morgan, Keith L. Nelson, G. A. Arbatov. Re-Viewing the Cold War: Domestic Factors and Foreign Policy in the East (Greenwood Publishing Group, 2000) page 82.

[144] "Reds Brainwash West's Defectors" New York Times March 24, 1955 page 6.

[145] Wolf, Markus and McElvoy, Anne. Man Without a Face (PublicAffairs 1999) pages 240-243.

[146] Radio Free Europe Research. Communists Set Up Demoralization Committees in East Germany to Undermine NATO April 13, 1956 Accessed From: http://storage.osaarchivum.org/low/ec/51/ec5110d1-8dfb-4649-892e-ad6d11fa88de_1.pdf

the policy of the most aggressive imperialist circles…We are registering changes in views on security policy within most social democratic and socialist parties and the trade-union federations under their influence. They are showing a readiness to cooperate with us on important issues related to ensuring peace und disarmament…the former, decades-long unity of the CDU/CSU, SPD and FDP on questions of military policy has largely collapsed on another issue beyond the talks on intermediate-range weapons. This has been made possible by the influence over many years of the peace policy of the socialist states, the growing influence of the GDR on the FRG's citizens, the pressure exerted by voters and members of the SPD, the peace movement, the German trade union federation, the activities of the GCP (German Communist Party in West Germany) but also by the influence of concrete vested interests on the part of a considerable portion of the bourgeoisie."

Honecker also observed that *"…the political forces in the FRG are becoming ever more polarized. We are finding that new opportunities are opening up for collaboration with the forces of reason on a social level: with representatives of the SPD, the Green Party, the trade unions, Christian youth and other circles, and with anti-war forces in the broadest sense of the word. This should be exploited to the greatest possible extent in order to influence the actions of the current government, which, after all, consists not only of the CDU/CSU but also the FDP."*[147]

Clearly, the SPD and the FDP absorbed much of the *"Kool Aid"* of détente and *Ostpolitik*. Anti-communism within these political sectors became severely compromised. Human rights violations and atrocities within the East German state were covered-up. Koehler wrote that *"the West German parties' fawning over Honecker during his 1987 state visit was not lost on the East German people: They were watching coverage of the events on television. They could see that the Social Democrats and many liberal Free Democrats were particularly anxious to please the DDR's leaders. The leading officials of those two parties had tried for years to have the Central Registration Office and its files on communist crimes destroyed. It is understandable, therefore, that most East Germans, even those who did not join the party, chose to accommodate the regime."*[148]

The DKP continued to be obedient lackeys of the East German SED. In fact, DKP militants comprised the activists which welcomed the visit of SED Chairman/East German dictator Honecker to West Germany in September 1987. At least 300 DKP activists chanted *"Welcome to the ambassador of peace and reason"* while in the presence of Honecker.[149]

The Peace Committee of the Federal Republic of Germany (FKdBD) received 100,000 West German Deutschmarks (DM) per month from the SED for peace activities in West Germany. The Secretary of the KPD lived in East Berlin-Pankow adjacent to the SED Politburo members. All KPD decisions had to be approved by the SED, who then dispatched delegates to KPD meetings. The Arbeitsbuero (Department for All-German Affairs) of the SED controlled the *"West Work"* of KPD front and mass organizations in West Germany. The FDGB sought to

---

[147] "Speech by Comrade Erich Honecker" October 22, 1985 Parallel History Project on Cooperative Security Accessed From:http://www.php.isn.ethz.ch/collections/colltopic.cfm?lng=en&id=19114&navinfo=14465

[148] Koehler, John O. Stasi: The Untold Story of the East German Secret Police (Basic Books, 2008) pages 24-26.

[149] Christensen, Anna. "Conservatives protest Honecker visit" United Press International September 9, 1987

create clandestine organizations in West Germany and sought to open relations with West German trade unions. The Arbeitsbuero employed 16,000 agents who worked out of East Berlin or were sent as Instrukteure to West Germany. The Independent Department of the Political Administration in the East German Ministry of Defense produced propaganda directed against Bundeswehr and NATO forces. Four million West German DM and 2.5 million East German Ostmarks were spent by the SED and KPD to weaken West German will towards resisting communism.[150]

The core of the West German peace movement was formed from the DKP. The DKP was funded by the East German SED with an annual income of 50 million DM to support its fronts and peace initiatives.[151] The Soviet Control Commission transmitted orders through Igor Glagolev to SED Secretary Hermann Axen to manipulate the West German pacifist movement called Ohne Uns (Without Us).[152] Wolf also revealed that the East Germans encouraged the formation of the German Union for Peace in 1968 by DKP officials.[153]

In 1974, the Committees for Peace, Disarmament and Cooperation (Komitees für Frieden, Abrustung und Zusammenarbeit or KOFAZ) was formed and controlled by high-level DKP leaders. Such DKP officials or front group leaders within the KOFAZ included Martha Buschmann of the executive board of the DKP, Klaus Mannhardt (former chairman of the DFG-VK), and Horst Trapp (German Peace Union). The Socialist German Worker Youth of the DKP was closely allied to KOFAZ. In the early 1980s, Mechthild Jansen, an official of the DKP-oriented Democratic Women's Initiative and a member of KOFAZ, initiated a campaign against women serving in the Bundeswehr.[154]

The violent anti-nuclear demonstration near Brokdorf (located near Hamburg) in 1976 was funded by East Germany. East Germany provided 100,000 DM to the anti-nuclear groups in West Germany. In mid- 1976, Gerhardt Schuerer, the Chairman of the East German State Planning Commission noted that *"disruptive activities against the construction of atomic plants in the capitalist West, especially in the Federal Republic, must be promoted. Trained provocation units (Stoergruppen) have been dispatched."*[155]

It was noted the German Peace Union (DFU) was subsidized with 5 million DM per year from the Stasi. The group KFAZ received cash from the Stasi and used this money to rent buses, print signs, and conduct mass protest appeals. Generals for Peace received hundreds of thousands DM per year from the Stasi.[156]

---

[150] USAREUR Intelligence Estimate – 1965 February 15, 1965 US National Archives, Records of the Army Staff Accessed From:http://www.php.isn.ethz.ch/collections/colltopic.cfm?lng=en&id=18593&navinfo=14968 (Choose Part 9)

[151] Vermaat, J.A. Emerson. "Moscow Fronts and the European Peace Movement" Problems of Communism November 1982 pages 43-56.

[152] Glagolev, Dr. Igor S. Post-Andropov Kremlin Strategy (Association for Cooperation of Democratic Countries, 1984) page 13.

[153] Wolf, Markus and McElvoy, Anne. Man Without a Face (PublicAffairs 1999) pages 270-271.

[154] Breyman, Steve. Movement Genesis: Social Movement Theory and the 1980s West German Peace Movement (Westview Press 1998) pages 90-94.

[155] Crozier, Brian. "Power and National Sovereignty" National Review February 2, 1979 page 167.

[156] Schweizer, Peter. Reagan's War (Random House LLC 2003)

In 1981, the Stasi outlined its policy of working with leftist and other subversive movements in West Germany. The Stasi instructed its agents to give material and political support to the peace movement, but not to attempt to lead it directly. The Stasi they had a sufficient number of pro-East German organizations within the West German peace movement to ensure that the pacifists served the interests of the Warsaw Pact. One Stasi order noted *"Members of the Bundeswehr the West German armed forces who question the sense of the planned armament measures are to be won over."* Former Stasi officer Guenter Bohnsack stated *"The Russians told us that we should find people in the West who would implement our ideas and tactical demands and would spread them in the West. The most obvious thing to do was to look around for soldiers who could speak competently about peace and war and, since soldiers can only talk after they have retired, we had the idea of looking for people who were retired and who wanted to be politically active. That's why we looked closely at NATO and that's when we came across General Bastian in Germany and the others."* The Stasi located 10 generals and decided to publish a book of which they would all be invited to contribute. Bohnsack stated: *"Out of this rather loose gathering grew a real movement. People telephoned each other, organized debates, talked to each other. This created a real power that was in line with Moscow's ideas and we always controlled this through our intelligence services in Moscow and East Berlin."*

Bohnsack commented further: *"There was a whole range of expenses which were paid jointly by Moscow and the GDR. I believe that some of the generals asked about the origin of the funds, and they asked very loudly at times, but one Dutch general replied that wherever it came from it served a good purpose."*[157]

The Stasi also sent from 1981 onwards $44,500 to the Generals for Peace and Disarmament (GPD). GPD opposed Western defense measures and apologized for the Soviet military buildup in Eastern Europe. The money was provided through an intermediary of Stasi/HVA General Markus Wolf.[158]

According to HVA General Markus Wolf, the anti-nuclear protests in the West which occurred in the 1970s and 1980s received financial support from the East. In 1968, the German Union for Peace (DFU) was formed by individuals connected with the DKP. A 1979 HVA/Stasi memo observed *"Among young people from well situated families a fundamental shift in values is under way. Personal advancement and material well-being are declining in importance for this section of society. Engagement in the wider questions of mankind, solidarity, and a 'we feeling' or being locked into a group sharing interests and ideals running contrary to those of the capitalist state are considered the truly worthwhile undertakings."*[159]

West German Leftists also cooperated with foreign governments in demonstrations against the United States and NATO presence in West Germany. Libya and PLO representatives worked with the DKP to create an *"international alliance"* against imperialism, former President Reagan, and the United States. The East Germans also passed money to the DKP for this and other related efforts. The head of the SPD youth organization Rudolf Hartung positively noted that *"Social Democrats and Communists demonstrate together against the alliance with the United States."*[160] In 1984, representatives from the communist Salvadoran terrorist FMLN, the

---

[157] Hilton, Isabel. "The Green with a Smoking Gun" The Independent April 26, 1994 page 1.
[158] "NATO Generals Were Manipulated by East Germany's Stasi: Report" Agence France Presse April 8, 2001
[159] Wolf, Markus and McElvoy, Anne. Man Without a Face (PublicAffairs 1999) pages 240-243.
[160] "Report PLO, Libya Link to Anti-Reagan Demos" United Press International June 2, 1982

DKP, and the ruling Sandinista party of Nicaragua participated in demonstrations in West Germany that opposed American policy in Central America.[161] The East Germans reported that North Korea had *"contact with Maoist and Trotskyite groups in the FRG and West Berlin"* in the early 1970s.[162]

The Green Party demanded that West Germany withdraw from NATO and abolish all uses of nuclear energy at their 1986 congress. The Green Party resolution specifically stated that there *"can be no peace with NATO - it is vital to weaken and abolish the alliance to achieve peace. NATO can no longer be reformed. What matters is the weakening of NATO as the alliance that has consistently promoted the arms race."*[163] Leading peace movement campaigner, anti-NATO activist, and Greens Party Bundestag Deputy Alfred Mechtersheimer maintained close ties with Qaddafi's Libya through a foundation based in Liechtenstein. This foundation was backed with $10 million in Libyan funds.[164]

By November 1984, West German Greens Party leader Antje Vollmer informed SED Politburo member Herbert Haber that he was comfortable with the SED and not *"with our own bourgeois parties."* An East German Stasi agent Dirk Schneider served as a member of the Bundestag from 1983 to 1985 in the Greens Party. He was also a Stasi agent who served the East Germans from 1975 to 1990. By November 1989, the Greens developed a fully pro-Soviet and pro-East German platform. By late 1989, the Greens Party called for respect for East Germany's *"independence,"* endorsed the notion that American militarism was the chief threat to peace, and called for West Germany to withdraw from NATO. The Greens also called for the closure of the anti-communist, American RIAS radio broadcasting system. The pro-Soviet, pro-East German bent of the Greens could be attributed to the influence of party members such as Dirk Schneider and Otto Schily.[165]

The East Germans also attempted to influence and recruit elements of the West German trade unions in an effort to gather intelligence on industries, position agents to sabotage factories and infrastructure, and to engage in strikes and political subversion to divide the public from the Bonn government. Since 1974, the headquarters of the East German dummy trade union FDGB received many West German visitors. The FDGB organized propaganda trips to East Germany by workers, trade unionists, and *"interested citizens,"* that were mainly from West Germany. During this period, over 130,000 guests visited East Germany through International e.V. Almost 17,000 traveled to East Germany alone under the auspices of the FDGB and International e.V. In 1988, the hard currency generated for the SED by these trips totaled DM 2.3 million.[166]

---

[161] Roby, Edward. "20 Injured in Anti-American Protests" United Press International November 3, 1984

[162] Armstrong, Charles K. Tyranny of the Weak (Cornell University Press 2013) page 1970.

[163] Markham, James M. "Green Party Asks Break with NATO" New York Times May 21, 1986 page 8.

[164] Marsh, David. "Greens Man In Row Over 'Links With Libya'" Financial Times March 28, 1989 page 4.

[165] Schmeidel, John Christian. Stasi: Shield and Sword of the Party (Routledge 2007) pages 131-132

[166] "FDGB Statement on its Foreign Currency Dealings" East German News Agency December 8, 1989

Even the Lyndon LaRouche movement based in the United States established its roots in West Germany. By 1973, some cadres from the LaRouchian National Caucus of Labor Committees (NCLC) recruited members in West Germany from the DKP's MBS Spartukus and the Trotskyite Communist organization called the Spartacus BL. They established the European Labor Committee (ELC), which became in 1974 the European Workers' Party (EAP). The ELC/EAP claimed to be more leftist that the established Left in West Germany. The EAP believed that the Rockefellers and Kissinger sought to plunge the world into a war and called for the "*reconstruction program for the world economy.*" The EAP also despised the SPD establishment in West Germany. In early 1975, the EAP in West Germany launched a campaign against former Chancellor and SPD leader Willi Brandt. The EAP dubbed him as a Nazi and a "*CIA-bootlicker.*" An EAP poster in the 1976 Bundestag campaign read "*we get 5% in the Bundestag or atomic war in 1977 is unavoidable.*"[167]

ELC/EAP chapters in West Germany totaled 150 members. During the 1975 West German state elections, the ELC called for the implementation of the following programs:

1) Increased production of tractors, farm machinery, and fertilizers.
2) Securing markets in COMECON and Third World countries by treaty.
3) The development of a Euro-Ruble market.

By early 1974, the ELC/EAP abandoned its anti-Soviet line and embraced a pro-Soviet position. In late 1975, the EAP called for cooperation with the USSR, hard-line pro-Soviet communist parties, and the left-wing elements of the West German SPD against the "*Maoist plague.*"[168] Clearly, the ELC/EAP would have cooperated with an East German/Soviet invasion of West Germany on the account of ideological compatibility.

The Soviets aggressively sought to revive the traditional entente between German extreme nationalists and Moscow through the good offices of East Germany. The SED and the Nazis possessed a common adherence to a variant of socialism and anti-capitalism. Both sought to fight against the West and disliked the Jews, either openly or under the guise of anti-Zionism. The dividing point between the National Socialists and the Communists was the basis of their respective socialisms. The collectivism/socialism of the Nazis was based on race, while the communists based their socialism on proletarian revolution. Pro-Soviet feelings within the Nazi Party never fully died in Germany, even after the Axis invasion of the USSR in June 1941. The Soviets and SED sought to capitalize on the residual sympathies for National Socialism and resentment towards Western defeat of the Third Reich and their subsequent occupation of the Western half of Germany. East German Foreign Minister Georg Dertinger noted to General Lucius Clay that "*Germany has in modern times produced only one truly great statesman. That was Bismarck. Bismarck understood that the future security and prosperity of Germany lay in an alliance with Russia and the development of the closest trade relations between the two countries. But Kaiser Wilhelm II was a fool who listened to stupid advisers and abandoned Bismarck's wise policies. So, came World War I and bitter defeat for Germany.*"[169]

---

[167] Mletzko, Matthias. The LaRouche-Organization: In the Gray Zone between Extremism, Cultism and Political Exoticism Accessed From: http://larouchedanger.com/html/greyzone_engl.html

[168] Central Intelligence Agency. The European Labor Committee Accessed From: http://laroucheplanet.info/pmwiki/downloads/CIA%20FOIA%20On%20ELC.pdf

[169] Clay, Lucius D. This Is Germany (Sloane NY 1950) pages 411-412.

The Soviets and the SED sought to recruit former extreme nationalists and Nazis in the East for their technical expertise, their commitment to a form of socialism, and to appeal to the latent anti-Western, militarist sentiments in both occupied zones of Germany. General Lucius Clay reported that *"The East German regime took the lead in embracing ex-Nazis, professional soldiers, and even Junker ex-landlords and industrialists -- if they were willing to join in the holy crusade for 'national unity.' All of them were told over and over again the story of how the long-range interests of Germany intertwined with those of the Soviet Union."*[170]

The political commissar of the Soviet Military Administration noted at a meeting of East German editors in Leipzig: *"This man (Pastor) Niemoller*[171] *is worth ten divisions to our cause."*[172] Soviet Marshal V.D. Sokolovsky declared in 1948: *"Among the former Nazis there are many skilled organizers and experts who are willing to cooperate with the democratic elements who are fighting for Germany's unity. If they do it honestly and loyally they must receive an opportunity."*[173] A Soviet general in the Soviet Occupation Zone in Germany (SBZ) told his East German subordinates that they *"should introduce internal order appropriate to the German tradition."*[174] Stalin himself wanted the SED to recruit *"patriotic elements"* to a *"fascist party"* especially among *"secondary figures of the former Nazi Party."* Stalin justified this policy on the grounds that the *"Nazis"* had *"come from out of the people… we must not forget that the elements of Nazism are alive not only in the bourgeois layers, but also among the working class and the petty bourgeoisie."* [175]

Former high-level American Communist Benjamin Gitlow reported that *"Selected German students, many of them former Nazis, officers in Hitler's armies and officials of his party, have been educated and trained by the thousands in the communist schools in Russia and sent back to Germany to serve the communist world superstructure in the hub of the world where the conflict between communism and European civilization takes on an acute form."*[176]

In 1948, it was reported that SS, *Kleinst Kampfverband der Kriegsmarine* (K Units), and paratroop units from the Third Reich were being recruited into the Soviet Zone's Volkspolizei units as *"champions of socialism."*[177]

---

[170] Ibid, pages 245-246.

[171] Niemoller was a national socialist-oriented pastor who later became famous for opposing the Nazis.

[172] Muhlen, Norbert. The Return of Germany: A Tale of Two Countries (H. Regnery Company Chicago 1953) pages 128-131

[173] Morrow, Edward A. "Russians End Denazifying Units, Declaring Fascism Is Thwarted" New York Times February 28, 1948 page 4.

[174] Hendrik, Paul. "'Ulbricht's Helpers:' The Role of Hitler's Army Generals in Former East Germany" April 25, 2001 Accessed From: http://www.wsws.org/articles/2001/apr2001/ss-a25.shtml

[175] Bolton, K.R. "Stalin's German Nationalist Party" Inconvenient History Volume 6 Number 1 2014 Accessed From: http://inconvenienthistory.com/archive/2014/volume_6/number_1/stalins_german_nationalist_party.php

[176] Gitlow, Benjamin. The Whole of the Their Lives (Charles Scribner's Sons New York 1948) pages 250-253.

[177] Middleton, Drew. "Soviet Organizes 400,000 Into German Police Force" New York Times October 7, 1948 page 1.

Reports surfaced in the hands of Western Allied authorities of the Soviet retention of ex-Nazis and war criminals in Eastern Zone of Germany. In 1949, the British revealed that Ernest Lohagen, president of the SED in Saxony, was a confidential agent in the Gestapo, while Professor Sedlaczek, works director of the Soviet Zone's largest iron works, was an *"armaments fuehrer"* of the largest steel works in Thale during World War II.[178]

The Soviets spirited Deputy Fuhrer Rudolf Hess out of Spandau Prison in 1952. Hess was requested to take over as head of the East German puppet organization for ex-Nazis, which was called the National Democratic Party. According to Otto Grotewohl, *"Hess…was to proclaim publicly that the socialism of which he had dreamed was being realized in East Germany."* Stalin believed that large numbers of Nazis in East and West Germany would unite behind the former Deputy-Fuhrer of the Third Reich. Hess replied that he could never trick Hitler in that manner after the Fuhrer's death.[179] However, it was reported that Hess *"welcomed… the efforts of the DDR and the Soviet Union to preserve German patriotism, and had listened attentively to what his interlocutors had to say on the programs of the political parties referred to…"*[180]

East German People's Police General Vincenz Mueller wrote in March 1952 in the <u>Berlin Tägliche Rundschau</u>[181] that *"today former members of the Nazi Party and former professional soldiers and officers occupy responsible positions in all branches of (East German) economic, political, and cultural life. They are men of good will fighting for a democratic united Germany."* The titular East German President Wilhelm Pieck noted in 1949 that *"For the enlistment of Nazis in our National Front, there is no other condition than their sincere will to fight for the unity and independence of Germany."* The ex-Nazis in the East German government and armed forces wrote chain letters to their counterparts in West Germany which stated: *"Why continue a hopeless struggle over there? Why emigrate to Egypt, Argentina, the Middle East as some of us have done? Come here; you'll find the old comrades, the old spirit, and the old ideals."*[182]

One SED functionary stated *"We must take these specialists away from the shovel and reinstate them where they are needed."* The main SED speaker at an economic conference in Leipzig in April 1947 urged that: *"We have the absolute duty of enlisting the cooperation of scientists, engineers, technicians, doctors, indeed all those men who are so urgently needed in economic life, above all when they were nominal PGs (Partei Gennossen or Party Comrades in the Nazis)."* Special and superior canteens were established for these specialists, while they had access to purchase goods at the elite Handelsorganisation (HO) stores.[183]

---

[178] "Find Nazis in Soviet Area" <u>New York Times</u> February 23, 1949 page 10.
[179] "One Night of Freedom Did Hess Nix Soviet Job Offer in '52?" <u>Philadelphia Daily News</u> September 4, 1987
[180] Bolton, K.R. "Stalin's German Nationalist Party" <u>Inconvenient History</u> Volume 6 Number 1 2014 Accessed From: http://inconvenienthistory.com/archive/2014/volume_6/number_1/stalins_german_nationalist_party.php
[181] Newspaper of the Soviet Control Commission in the Soviet Zone of Germany.
[182] Muhlen, Norbert. <u>The Return of Germany: A Tale of Two Countries</u> (H. Regnery Company Chicago 1953) pages 70-72.
[183] Pritchard, Gareth. <u>The Making of the GDR</u> (Manchester University Press 2004) pages 195-196.

By the 1950s, the ranks of the East German armed forces, SED party apparatus, and other official institutions found themselves flooded with ex-Nazis, war criminals, and Wehrmacht officers. The East Germans valued their intelligence, propaganda, and economic expertise from the National Socialist dictatorship. SS General Hans Rattenhuber became a senior political police official in East Germany. Abwehr Lt. Gen. Rudoplh Bamler became an agent of the GRU and a department head at Stasi Headquarters in East Berlin. Johann Sanitzer was an anti-Jewish expert in the Gestapo in Vienna who later was employed as a Volkspolizei Major in Erfurt in East Germany. SS Captain Louis Hagemeister became chief police interrogator in Schwerin. SS Sturmbannfuhrer Heidenreich became the official liaison between the Stasi and the Central Committee of the SED.[184] Former Nazi Dr. Gunter Kertzscher, was employed as the Deputy Editor in Chief of Neues Deutschland, which was the official newspaper of the SED. Former Nazi Hans W. Aust became the Editor in Chief Deutsche Aussenpolitik which was the foreign policy journal of East Germany. Former Nazi propagandist Kurt Blecha became the Chief of Press Service in East Germany. Horst Drebler-Andreb, was a Nazi Party member who was also the head of the German Broadcasting Service in Goebbels' Propaganda Ministry. After the defeat of Nazi Germany, Drebler-Andreb became a leading SED propagandist. Kurt Schumann, President of the East German Supreme Court formerly served as a Nazi Judge Advocate. Professor Herbert Kroger was a former SS sergeant who was attached to the Security Division (SD). He later became the Rector of the Walter Ulbricht Academy of Political and Legal Sciences. Curt Sauberlich was a Deputy in the East German puppet legislature called the Volkskammer. Formerly, Sauberlich was a former SS First Lieutenant in the SD. Ernst Grossman, was a SS Death's Head officer who became a member of the SED Central Committee. Dr. Adolf Otto, was member of the Presidential Board of the German Peace Council and former Nazi.[185] Kurt Ball, was the Editor of SS newspaper Hammer and writer for Schwarze Korps. Later, Ball became a writer for East German state-owned newspapers and an official in the propaganda departments in East Germany. Liselotte Ottiug was in involved in the administration of the SS *"sex farms"* and later became the head of the culture and publicity department of the puppet East German Liberal Party. Gerhard Kegel was a former Gestapo informer at the German Embassy in occupied Poland and later became an official in the East German Foreign Ministry who participated in international conferences.[186] Hermann Klenner was an East German vice president of the UN Commission on Human Rights who almost became that organization's chairman. He was a Nazi Party member and enrolled in the Hitler Youth.[187]

It was revealed that Hans Sommer of the SS was recruited by the Stasi to spy on right wing politicians in West Germany and Italy. Sommer's previous, sordid claim to fame was his activities of bombing Paris synagogues during the German occupation of France. Gestapo officer at Auschwitz Josef Settnik was offered a position with the Stasi in 1964. Gestapo officer Willy Laeritz turned over his interrogation expertise to the Stasi after World War II *"to support our*

---

[184] Simpson, Christopher. Blowback (Collier Books-Macmillan 1989) pages 78-79.
[185] Lewis, Fulton. "East German Red Party Nazi Haven" Chronicle Telegram July 24, 1961 page 26.
[186] "Ex-Nazis Hold Key Jobs in East Germany" Winnipeg Free Press January 2, 1969 page 24.
[187] "U.S. Joins Bid to Block Job for Alleged Ex-Nazi" The San Francisco Chronicle May 26, 1986

fight for peace and socialism."[188] Dr. Rosemarie Albrecht served in the East German Jena Academy as a deacon and treated the SED Chairman Walter Ulbricht. She even won the *"People's Doctor of Outstanding Merit"* from the ruling SED. Dr. Albrecht was previously involved in the Nazi euthanasia programs of the 1930s.[189]

Various ex-Nazis such as Max Volmer, R. Dopel, P. Thiessen, and Gustav Hertz served in the Soviet and East German nuclear programs. Specifically, these ex-Nazi scientists were employed in Soviet programs to develop weapons grade uranium. Baron von Ardenne became later an East German electronics specialist. Thiessen was previously an ardent Nazi and an expert in chemistry and explosives who received the Golden Party Medal by the Nazis. Professor Volmer worked for the Soviets because he believed that Western Germany would be despoiled by the Morganthau Plan. A German physicist named Heinz Barwich traveled to the USSR in June 1945 in order to seek paid employment.[190]

Even certain Nazi-aligned literary and theatrical figures shifted their loyalties to the Soviets and the KPD. Gerhart Hauptmann was an ardent Socialist and playwright who later supported the Nazis. He was close with Goebbels and Hans Johst. The Soviets later recruited Hauptmann in 1945 and allowed him to produce plays in East Berlin. In October 1945, Hauptmann stated in a message to the KPD-dominated Kulturbund for the Democratic Revival of Germany that he wished it every success in bringing about the *"spiritual rebirth"* of the German people.[191]

Even more grotesque were Nazis who served in the official *"anti-fascist"* and Jewish community organizations. A Nazi SA trooper became the spokesperson of the Jewish community of Zittau in East Germany. Ex-Nazis also became members of the GDR Coalition of the Victims of the Nazi Regime.[192]

The East Germans and the Soviets also sought to recruit ex-Nazis and war criminals in postwar Austria. In 1950, sections of the Independent Party in Austria joined up with the pro-Soviet National League led by former SS officer Dr. Slavik. The National League was a repository for Nazi war criminals from the SS, SD, Gestapo, Party functionaries, and officers in the various paramilitary groups of the Third Reich. Dr. Slavik bragged that he was an old guard Austrian Nazi who was part of their original, illegal network of the 1920s and 1930s Dr. Slavik later appealed to former SS and Nazi officers for an *"understanding with the East."*[193]

Dr. Slavik was in touch with the East German front for ex-Nazis located in Dresden. Austrian National League members were trained by the East German Volkspolizei in East Berlin and dispatched back to their native country. Austrian Nazi police councilor Johann Sannitzer was

---

[188] Connoly, Kate. "Nazis spied for East Germany" Daily Telegraph November 1, 2005 page 16.

[189] Paterson, Tony. "Stasi Files Hid Proof That Showed Doctor Was Nazi Murderer" The Independent February 14, 2004 page 30.

[190] Albrecht, Ulrich. The Soviet Armaments Industry (Harwood Academic Publishers, 1993) pages 119-120.

[191] Shirer, William L. The Rise and Fall of the Third Reich (Simon and Schuster, 1990) page 243.

[192] Broder, Henryk M. A Jew in the New Germany (University of Illinois Press, 2004) page 86.

[193] "Vienna Ex-Nazi Group Joins Camp of Soviet" New York Times May 15, 1950 page 3.

one of the National League officers that were trained and recruited to join the East German Volkspolizei as an officer.[194]

The East Germans even exported ex-Nazi expertise to its ideological allies abroad. Over 250 ex-Gestapo officers were dispatched by the East Germans to leftist or Marxist regimes such as Sukarno's Indonesia, Egypt, Syria, and Ghana.[195]

New neo-Nazi groups sprouted up in West Germany shortly after the end of World War II. While ideologically anti-Marxist, the West German neo-Nazis retained an attachment to a heterodox form of socialism and some were even open to outright cooperation with Moscow and East Berlin. Some were even funded by the Soviets and East Germans. The neo-Nazi Socialist Reich Party (SRP) in West Germany supported the notion that *"the state will enforce the supremacy of the commonweal over individual interests"* and favored what it termed *"folk socialism."*

One of the SRP leaders named Fritz Dorls observed that *"When Hitler and Stalin concluded their pact in 1939, the two national socialisms of our time joined each other forever in the logical line of history; for both had basically the same ideals and the same goals. America was aware of the fact that this alliance meant death to its capitalist aspirations and its lust for power. Therefore, Wall Street dispatched its secret agents to Hitler and to Stalin, and these American devils actually succeeded in breaking up the pact and the friendship of the two great men, and in driving the two great systems against each other…The breaking of the Nazi-Soviet Pact was the greatest catastrophe of the century. We must never let it happen again; Nazi Germany and Soviet Russia must stand together."*[196]

Elements of the West German neo-Nazi movement openly indicated their desire to cooperate with the Soviets in the event of an invasion of West Germany. Dorls noted that *"If war comes, we must greet the Russians with open arms, and let them pass through our country. If we participated, the Amis and the Russians would throw their atom bombs on our poor country and destroy us forever. A new National Socialist Germany leading Western Europe will, as a third force between East and West, ally herself with the Soviet bloc, which it recognizes as Eastern National Socialism. As its ally rather than its satellite, new Nazi Germany would share the world with Soviet Russia."*[197]

During a 1948 meeting outlining the European Liberation Front, American neo-fascist activist and writer Francis Parker Yockey supported the creation of *"secret partisans in Western Germany who would be prepared to collaborate with the Soviet Military Authorities in action against the Western occupying powers."*

SRP leader and former pro-Hitler Wehrmacht General Otto Ernst Remer noted that *"Instead of letting our women and children be overrun by the Russians and our men bled to death in the new Maginot Line, we should stretch out our arms so that the Russians can march as speedily as possible through Germany."*[198]

---

[194] MacCormac, John. "Soviet Sponsoring Party in Austria" <u>New York Times</u> May 7, 1950 page 12.
[195] "Ex Gestapo Men Key East German Aid" <u>Lima News</u> June 8, 1966 page 18.
[196] Muhlen, Norbert. <u>The Return of Germany: A Tale of Two Countries</u> (H. Regnery Company Chicago 1953) pages 60-68.
[197] Ibid.
[198] Coogan, Kevin. <u>Dreamer of the Day</u> (Autonomedia 1999) pages 400-401.

The SRP pledged to *"show the Russians the way to the Rhine"* in the event of a Soviet invasion. SRP militants would *"post themselves as traffic policemen spreading their arms so that the Russians can find their way through Germany as quickly as possible."*[199]

Eberhardt Stern, the former chairman of the Berlin branch of the SRP, reported that the third chairman of the party, Count Westarp, received the sum of 32,000 DM from the SED office in East Berlin. Another SRP official, Heinrich Keseberg, published a document which revealed that Dorls requested additional support from the Polish-Soviet agent in Lodz, Colonel Stanislav Dombrovski. In November 1951, the president of the small Racist Liberty Party (Voelkische Freiheitspartei), Alfred Formann was a former official Nazi party speaker of the Propaganda Ministry. Formann urged that *"we old Nazis must remember our mission"* and called for an alliance with the Soviet Union. They sang the Horst Wessel Lied and the song *"Do you see the dawn in the East?"*[200] In 1951, Erhard Scholten, president of the Racist Action Group (Voelkische Aktionsgruppe) noted to a group of former Hitler Youth leaders that *"Our aim is a new and unified Reich allied with Russia, that traditional partner of the German people."*[201]

In 1957, former Nazi fanatic and Propaganda Ministry official Johann von Leers noted that *"The brutal Jewish tyranny in Western Germany backed by the American government forces more and more patriots either to emigrate mostly to Islamic countries or to search refuge in the communist part of Germany…The monkey love of the USA government for the Jews isolates the Americans both in Germany and in the Near East. On the other hand the Russians are clever enough to appeal to the sound anti-Jewish feeling of the peoples."*[202]

Wolf Schenke, former chief editor of the Hitler Youth publication <u>Wille und Macht</u> and a Far East Correspondent for the <u>Volkischer Beobachter</u>, organized the West German Congress Against Re-Militarization in 1951. Delegates to the West German Congress Against Re-Militarization included members of the Bruderschaft, SRP, and fronts for the KPD and SPD. The Deutsche Reichs Party (DRP) blasted the European Defense Community as an *"instrument of Jewish imperialism."* Other ex-Nazis made contact with the East German news agency ADN in the early 1950s. Richard Scheringer was a former Nazi who became a KPD/SED functionary. Others reportedly signed the Soviet front World Peace Council's Stockholm Appeal in 1950 and conferred with Soviet military authorities in Karlshorst.

In 1952, the West German Interior Minister reported that the SRP received Soviet funding. SRP sources claimed that the party received substantial support from the West Kommission of the East German SED. A pro-neutralist meeting in Wiesbaden included SRP leaders like Fritz Dorls and representatives from Neutrales Deutschland, a front for the KPD.[203] Remer and the SRP secretly negotiated with Soviet authorities in East Germany. Remer recollected that *"I sent my people there…They were all received at the Soviet headquarters in Pankow."* The Soviets then remitted financial support to the SRP.[204]

---

[199] Lee, Martin A. <u>The Beast Reawakens</u> (Taylor & Francis 1999) page 65.
[200] Muhlen, Norbert. <u>The Return of Germany: A Tale of Two Countries</u> (H. Regnery Company Chicago 1953) pages 60-68.
[201] Ibid.
[202] Coogan, Kevin. <u>Dreamer of the Day</u> (Autonomedia 1999) pages 194-195.
[203] Ibid, pages 400-402.
[204] Lee, Martin A. "Strange Ties: The Stasi and the Neo-Fascists" <u>Los Angeles Times</u> September 10, 2000 Accessed From: <u>http://articles.latimes.com/2000/sep/10/opinion/op-18655/2</u>

Even during the Brezhnev-Gorbachev era, elements of the West German neo-Nazi movement retained their attachment to Soviet interests. In 1983, Remer and his German Freedom Movement noted that the German Federal Republic *"would not be used as the tip of the NATO spear…We will not participate in a NATO war against Russia…We have to realize and act accordingly, like Bismarck did, that Russia is the superpower in this gigantic Eurasian continent, to which we belong geographically, geopolitically and economically, and even culturally… We are, like Bismarck, for a close collaboration with Russia in politics, economy, culture, science, technology, and research."* Remer facilitated the purchase of 4,000 pistols by Castro's Cuba in 1962.[205]

In 1990, General Remer noted: *"We Germans must leave the NATO alliance. We must be militarily independent. We must create a nuclear-free zone. We must come to an understanding with the Russians. That is, we must obtain reasonable borders from the Russians. They are the only ones that can do that. The Americans don't have any influence at all in that regard. In return, we will guarantee to buy (Russian) raw materials, and cooperate on hundreds of projects with the Russians, and that will eliminate our unemployment. All this has nothing to do with ideology. The Russians are so economically backward that they will readily and happily agree to this, and they'll be free of ideology."* Remer reported that he also met with the Soviet Ambassador in Bonn, Valentin Falin and the Soviet Embassy press secretary for friendly exchanges and open conversations.[206]

Even the National Democratic Party (NPD) promoted a West German withdrawal from NATO and guarded negotiations with the Soviet Union. While the NPD was ideologically anti-communist, its leaders admired the USSR for its military power and usage of nationalist themes in its propaganda and ideology.[207] The NPD leader Adolf von Thadden praised the Soviet campaign against the Jews and Zionism in August 1978. He stated that *"only the Soviets will be seen to hold out any promise to wreak vengeance on the Jews."*[208] The NPD also called for the withdrawal of West Germany from NATO and the development of a powerful army. The NPD admitted that *"We know that we must negotiate with the Kremlin."*[209]

The NPD rejected liberal capitalism and communism and supported National Socialist collectivism. The NPD asserted that *"In economic practice all doctrines of the capitalist, liberal, and Marxist brand have proved themselves insufficient…The goal of the National Democratic economic policy is the synthesis of entrepreneurial freedom and social obligation."*[210] The NPD was also hostile to American foreign investments in West Germany. Its manifesto revealed that

---

[205] Bolton, K.R. "Stalin's German Nationalist Party" Inconvenient History Volume 6 Number 1 2014 Accessed From: http://inconvenienthistory.com/archive/2014/volume_6/number_1/stalins_german_nationalist_party.php

[206] "An Interview with General Otto Ernst Remer" Journal of Historical Review Spring 1990 Accessed From: http://www.ihr.org/jhr/v10/v10p108_Schoeman.html

[207] Stolley, Richard B. "A Son of the Junkers, To Whom Nationalism Is Glory and Hope" Life Magazine July 19, 1968 page 46.

[208] "Neo-Nazi Glee at Soviet Anti-Semitism" Volume 13 Issue 2 Patterns of Prejudice 1979 pages 29-30.

[209] Nagle, John David. The National Democratic Party (University of California Press 1970) pages 114-115.

[210] Ibid, page 114.

the NPD would *"guard against foreign control by foreign capital and against the selling out our basic industries to world concerns."*[211] The NPD campaigned on slogans such as *"Work for Germans first"* and *"Big capital destroys jobs."* According to a BND report, the purpose of the NPD was to *"build a new Germany out of the rubble of liberal capitalism."*[212] The NPD also advocated the conversion of independent labor unions into arms of the state and the banning of strikes and lockouts. The NPD also desired strict protectionist policies and an autarkic economy for West Germany.[213]

The German People's Union (DVU) of Gerhard Frey supported an alliance with Red China against the United States and the Soviet Union. Apparently, the DVU took the Sino-Soviet *"split"* at face value. However, my book Golitsyn Vindicated clearly documented that Moscow and Beijing cooperated on a number of issues and remained united against capitalism, imperialism, and the United States. The DVU called for closer West German-Red Chinese trade relations. It also promised that a DVU government would *"incorporate China into our political calculations."* The DVU also indicated that *"in their efforts to secure equal rights and self-determination, the Chinese deserve our fullest sympathy."*[214]

Various West German neo-Nazis and nationalist conservatives supported the pro-Soviet dictatorship in Iraq under Saddam Hussein. Neo-Nazi leader Michael Kuhnen contacted the Iraqi Embassy in Bonn to raise an anti-Zionist legion (called the International Freedom Corps) to fight against the United States. This legion was to be trained and funded by the Saddam regime. Kuhnen commented that Iraq and West German neo-Nazis possessed ideological commonalities: *"We have common ideals-the creation of living spaces for different people and races in accordance with their own culture and tradition."* He claimed that the Arab radicals were not communists, but nationalists *"just like we are."* Kuhnen believed that Iraq and the West German neo-Nazis had the same enemies: *"the United States and its backers, the Zionist forces."* Members of the International Freedom Corps strutted in Baghdad and donned SS uniforms.[215] Iraqi Minister of Information Abdel Lateef Jassem also addressed these neo-Nazis while wearing their SS uniforms.[216] Kuhnen also praised the Iraqi SCUD missile attacks on Israel. The Republikaner Party dispatched a representative to Baghdad, where he was warmly received by Iraqi Baathist Socialist officials. In the *"post"*-Cold War era, the DVU called for a German withdrawal from NATO and close ties with the Russian Federation. DVU leaders also supported Saddam Hussein and opposed American intervention to expel Iraqi troops.[217]

---

[211] Ibid, page 86.

[212] Lee, Martin A. "Former Left-Wing Extremist, German Extremist Horst Mahler Switches to Neo-Nazi National Democratic Party" SPLC Intelligence Report Accessed From: https://www.splcenter.org/fighting-hate/intelligence-report/2015/former-left-wing-german-extremist-horst-mahler-switches-neo-nazi-national-democratic-party

[213] Nagle, John David. The National Democratic Party (University of California Press 1970) pages 114-115.

[214] Aronsfeld, C.C. "Right Wing Flirtation with a Chinese Alliance" Patterns of Prejudice Volume 3 Issue 4 1969 page 16.

[215] Between Iraq and a Hard Place, Part 3 Accessed From: http://spitfirelist.com/for-the-record/ftr-380-between-iraq-and-a-hard-place-pt-3/

[216] Millar's Rent a Nazi Accessed From: http://www.constitution.org/ocbpt/ocbpt_04.htm

[217] Between Iraq and a Hard Place, Part 3 Accessed From: http://spitfirelist.com/for-the-record/ftr-380-between-iraq-and-a-hard-place-pt-3/

Various West German leftists moved into the neo-Nazi scene. Former Baader-Meinhof Gang attorney and collaborators Horst Mahler became involved with the NPD. Mahler praised the al-Qaeda attacks on the World Trade Center and Federal buildings in 2001. Mahler also served as a Stasi collaborator from 1967 to 1970. Mahler himself admitted that he remained true to elements of his Marxist past: *"You have to see it dialectically. One changes, and at the same time one remains the same."*[218] Rainer Langhans, prominent ex-member of *"Kommune 1"* urged *"We must be the better fascists, because in my view a fascist is somebody who of course wants to have heaven on earth, somebody who wants something good. In this viewpoint, Hitler of course as a great teacher for all of us, and nobody will be able to reject this. In this special case of spirituality I would say: Hitler is a failed spiritualist who had that what belongs to the inner levels on his outer levels."* Reinhold Oberlercher was the leading (German Socialist Students Organization (SDS) activist in Hamburg and a chief theoretician of the German SDS. He then became involved with the neo-Nazis and called for the establishment of a *"Fourth Reich."* Gunther Maschke, a former SDS member in Frankfurt, became a writer for neo-Nazi publications in the 1980s. Mahler, Maschke, and Oberlercher wrote in their *"Canonical Declaration concerning the Movement of 1968"* that *"the movement of the years around 1968 stood up neither for capitalism, neither for Third World or Eastern, nor for Western values, but solely for the right of every people of national-revolutionary and social-revolutionary self-liberation."*[219]

Elements of former Nazi circles in West Germany even mimicked communist tactics in colonizing opposing political parties that governed from Bonn. Clearly, this was an effort to take over West Germany from within, via concurrent uses of democratic and deceptive strategies. Former top Nazi and the post-Goebbels head of the Propaganda Ministry Werner Naumann noted *"In order to enable National Socialists…to gain influence over the political events, they should join the FDP, infiltrate it, and capture its leadership. He (Achenbach) demonstrates with a few examples how easy that would be. We could inherit the entire Land executive committee organization with no more than 200 members."* Naumann's circle of Nazis maintained ties to a group of SS officers that were sentenced by West Germany as communist spies.[220] Hence, it is possible that a Nazi takeover of West Germany through a heavily penetrated FDP and other democratic parties would result in, at least temporarily, a pro-Moscow posture in Bonn.

The neo-Nazi movement in the 1980s also continued their vitriol against the United States, NATO, and the Bonn government. West German Interior Minister Friedrich Zimmermann reported in 1984 that neo-Nazis displayed *"nationalist neutralism that often have aggressive, anti-American features. This nationalist, neutralist idea that aims at a reunified Greater Germany increasingly is showing features friendly to the Soviet Union is so because extreme right-wing circles believe a neutral, reunified Germany would be in the interest of the Soviet Union."* Two West German neo-Nazi leaflets called for: *"To defend the Fatherland today means actively to oppose the American war policy and the use of German soldiers for the goals of U.S. imperialism."* Other West German neo-Nazi flyers exhorted *"Stop re-armament. Get out*

---

[218] Pidd, Helen. "Baader-Meinhof terrorist may have worked for the Stasi" <u>The Guardian</u> August 1, 2011 Accessed From: http://www.theguardian.com/world/2011/aug/01/baader-meinhof-gang-founder-stasi

[219] "Horst Mahler: The Role of a Sad Sack" Accessed From: http://www.nettime.org/Lists-Archives/nettime-l-0010/msg00067.html

[220] Coogan, Kevin. <u>Dreamer of the Day</u> (Autonomedia 1999) pages 372-373.

of NATO. Down with nuclear missiles. Get the occupiers out." In 1983, Otto Ernst Remer noted: *"Who allies himself with the U.S.A. is lost. Who cooperates with the Soviet Union will survive and be victorious."*[221]

The West German neo-Nazi group VSBD-PdA spray painted slogans such as *"Down with the Ban on the KPD"* and *"Death to Fascism."* Left wing groups reportedly scrawled *"Blood must flow, plenty of it, and thick, we shit on the Jewish Republic."* One VSBD-PdA leader commented on leftist/neo-Nazi collaboration: *"Our cooperation is successful in other ways as well."* This cooperation included terror training and intelligence sharing. Volker Heidel of the German Socialist Party noted: *"We are not so far apart ideologically…Our common goal is the destruction of society. We want to develop a basic strategy of resistance and liberation."* Manfred Roeder of the Deutsche Aktionsgruppe supported *"the establishment of the first radical democratic and anti-imperialist state on German soil."* Michael Kuhnen of the Action Front of National Socialists admitted *"We always said we were socialists"* and supported the Greens Party and other leftist groups in opposing the deployment of Pershing and Cruise missiles on West German soil. Jailed neo-Nazi terrorists Odfried Hepp and Walter Kaxel stated in a letter that *"We can be gratified that there is a wall running through Germany. It at least ensures the survival of 17 million healthy Germans in the eastern part of the country. The minds and souls of the people here in the West are in the process of stultification…Forward in the anti-imperialist struggle."* Hepp also stated: *"We think everyone is justified in this struggle. We only have a chance if the rightists and leftists come together."*[222]

The Stasi also had close ties to the West German neo-Nazi group, Hoffman Wehrsportgruppe (Hoffman Military Sports Group), which was formed in the 1970s. One ex-Stasi official noted that *"We had an especially dense network of agents in this group…It ensured that we were able to steer the activities of these right-wing radicals in the right direction and never against East Germany."*[223]

In the post-1990 era, a number of leftwing neo-Nazis and traditional Hitler sympathizers exhibited solidarity with North Korea. This translated into political ties with North Korean diplomats resident in Germany. The NPD in eastern Germany (Saxony) maintained ties with the North Korean Embassy in Berlin starting in 1998. By the late 1990s, the Anti-Imperialist Platform (AIP) developed close sympathies with the North Koreans. The AIP was formed by the former Stalinist Communist-turned neo-Nazi Michael Koth. It took an anti-US, anti-Israel line that was sympathetic to communist and collectivist nationalist North Korea, Syria, Belarus, Iran, and Venezuela. The AIP disseminated its propaganda to the North Korean news agency, the KCNA. In 2012, Koth was invited to the North Korean Embassy in Berlin to celebrate the 100th birthday of communist dictator Kim Il Sung. Koth was also the head of the German-Korean Friendship Association in the 1990s, which distributed North Korean propaganda in neo-Nazi circles. Tobias Dondelinger, the author of the German language blog Nordkorea-info, observed: *"Many of the Nazis, which belong to the pro-NK faction are born in the former German Democratic Republic (GDR or East Germany), which was an ideological ally to North*

---

[221] Fleming, Joseph. "Neo-Nazis Appeal for Left-Wing Support, Report Says" United Press International April 7, 1984

[222] Hoffman, Bruce. "Right Wing Terrorism in Europe Since 1980" October 1984 Accessed From: http://www.rand.org/pubs/papers/2005/P7029.pdf

[223] Lee, Martin A. "Strange Ties: The Stasi and the Neo-Fascists" Los Angeles Times September 10, 2000 Accessed From: http://articles.latimes.com/2000/sep/10/opinion/op-18655

Korea...Some of them were mid-level officials of the GDR-Regime and thereby made contacts to the North Korean embassy in Berlin. After the end of the GDR, some of these ex-functionaries changed to the right political wing and even tried to push the major Nazi Party NPD into official contacts with North Korea...They are trying to sell brown ideas masked as red ideology...So, in my opinion, the adoration of North Korea by German Nazis can be explained through a mixture of ideological analogies and unique historical constellations."[224] German neo-Nazis also expressed admiration for Putin's Russia. For example, former NPD head Udo Voigt traveled to Russia for a conference in March 2015. This convention of neo-Nazis, extreme nationalists, and white nationalists was known as the *"Russian International Conservative Forum."* It received support from the Putin dictatorship. Conference guests were described as being opponents of European governments that were *"US puppets."*[225] The NPD itself observed that *"A spiritual and national renaissance of Europe can only be built on the foundation of strong Russo-German friendship."*[226] Hans-Gunther Eisener, the Chairman of the NPD, even noted that his party and the old East Germany held common ideological viewpoints: *"What is particularly important for East Germans is order, diligence, cleanliness. Values like liberty and tolerance hardly exist in their consciousness. The citizens still remember a society, where the collective meant more than the individual."* Eisener also admitted that the NPD maintained links with the neo-communist Party for Democratic Socialism (PDS) and nations like Red China and North Korea.[227]

Despite its professed anti-racism and internationalism, the East German SED dictatorship opposed Zionism, maintained anti-Jewish tendencies, and occasionally lapsed into racism during times of economic stress. As reported by Rasmussen, *"...racism was far from eradicated in East Germany, despite SED propaganda and testimonials from some African American visitors. The average East German still held on to their pre-1945 views on race, some in defiance of the SED's anti-racist rhetoric and others because it was a worldview to which they attributed a great deal of merit. Even within the ranks of the SED, racism remained entrenched among some of the Party's functionaries."*[228]

For example, in late 1989, the Krenz regime launched *"a xenophobic campaign against foreigners blaming them for shortages of consumer goods."* Apparently, this SED propaganda

---

[224] Young, Benjamin R. "The German Neo-Nazi fascination with North Korea" <u>NKNews.org</u> December 3, 2013 Accessed From: http://www.academia.edu/5349165/The_German_Neo-Nazi_Fascination_with_North_Korea

[225] Goble, Paul. "Russia Hosting Europe's Neo-Nazis, Nationalists and Anti-Semites, Putin Supporters All" <u>Interpreter Magazine</u> March 22, 2015 Accessed From: http://www.interpretermag.com/russia-hosting-europes-neo-nazis-nationalists-and-anti-semites-putin-supporters-all/

[226] Harzinger, Richard. "Europe's Extreme Right And Left United In Support Of Putin" <u>Worldcrunch</u> May 11, 2014 Accessed From: http://www.worldcrunch.com/opinion-analysis/europe-039-s-extreme-right-and-left-united-in-support-of-putin/russia-extremism-nationalism-ukraine-conflict/c7s15880/

[227] Kupferberg, Feiwel. <u>The Rise and Fall of the German Democratic Republic</u> (Transaction Publishers 2002) page 168.

[228] Natalia King Rasmussen. "Friends of Freedom, Allies of Peace: African Americans, the Civil Rights Movement, and East Germany, 1949-1989" Boston College Electronic Thesis or Dissertation, 2014 Accessed From: https://dlib.bc.edu/islandora/object/bc-ir:104045/datastream/PDF/view

campaign was effective with average East Germans.[229] Even in the early days of Soviet occupation in eastern Germany, anti-Semitism reared its ugly head. Both communist and Nazi anti-Semitism were conjoined together by a mutual anti-capitalism. In October 1945, the East Berlin SED cadre chief Fritz Reuter opposed financial restitution to Holocaust victims on the grounds that Jews were money-grubbing. He also claimed that the Jews were part of the petty-bourgeois and opposed to the working class. In 1949, the SED journal Einheit alleged that *"cosmopolitanism (i.e. Jews)"* was characterized by the negative image of *"the money man"* and *"the most complete image of capitalist exploitation."*[230] The anti-Semitism in East Germany only increased during the period of the early 1950s. When an East German SED official of Jewish birth named Paul Merker was arrested by the Stasi, he was alleged to have conspired to *"sell the DDR off to the Jews."* Merker was mocked as the *"king of the Jews"*, *"bought by the Jews,"* and the *"servant of the Jews."*[231] East German SED officials also arguably used coded anti-black racist terms when they denounced American music such as jazz, samba, and boogie woogie. Racialist terms that the SED utilized to describe such music included *"decadent," "primitivism," "American cultural barbarism,"* and *"public displays of sexual drives."*[232] These attacks started in the late 1940s and included cartoons which negatively accentuated Negroid features of jazz and rock n' roll enthusiasts and dancers. These cartoons portrayed lovers of jazz and rock n' roll with big lips and wide noses.[233] Guest workers from Asian and African allies of East Germany were often ostracized by the local population and paid low wages.[234] These laborers, totally 90,000 were *"quarantined like the slave labor that, in effect, they were."*[235] The Third World foreign guest workers were tightly controlled and monitored by the Stasi. Their labor terms were restricted to three year contracts with allied communist regimes such as Cuba, Vietnam, Angola, and Mozambique. Most guest workers lived in harsh circumstances and confined to single sex dormitories. East German citizens were not allowed to enter the ghettos set aside for the Third World guest workers. Sexual relations led to deportation of the Third World guest worker in question and the murder of the mixed race child by abortion.[236] A former Nigerian Communist Gilbert Ofodile, who was resident in East Germany, recalled that East German women were forced to abort babies after they were impregnated by males from Third World nations: *"…Mr. A.B. Brown, from South West Africa…was to terminate by abortion the pregnancy for which he was responsible and owned up to. Mr. Brown was forced to talk the girl into terminating the pregnancy by abortion by the Union of Journalists, this time headed by Miss Schön, for racial reasons. This young man had a girl friend by the name of Renate, who wanted to marry him and*

---

[229] Zatlin, Jonathan R. The Currency of Socialism (Cambridge University Press 2008) pages 335-336.

[230] LaPorte, Norman and Dennis, Mike. State And Minorities In Communist East Germany (Berghahn Books 2013) page 35.

[231] Herf, Jeffrey. Divided Memory (Harvard University Press, 1997) pages 144-145.

[232] Moeller, Robert G. West Germany Under Construction (University of Michigan Press, 1997) pages 387-388.

[233] Junker, Detlef. The United States and Germany in the Era of the Cold War, 1945-1990: A Handbook (Cambridge University Press) page 440.

[234] Brinks, Jan Herman. Children of a New Fatherland (I.B.Tauris 1999) page 24.

[235] Kramer, Jane. The Politics of Memory: Looking for Germany in the New Germany (Random House 1996) page 219.

[236] "Gastarbeiter" Accessed From: https://en.wikipedia.org/wiki/Gastarbeiter

get out of East Germany with him. If he liked, he could leave her alone on their getting out of East Germany, but if he wanted her, she was ready to live with him anywhere outside East Germany as his wife. Mr. Brown first resisted the pressure to get the girl (to) commit abortion, but when he was reminded that he was a refugee and that he got into East Germany without a passport and further, if he refused he would be flown to the South African Government, he had no alternative but to make her have an abortion...We boys saw the incident (as a form of) calculated racial hatred. Because before the incident they had warned us times without number to keep clear of the girls who were employed in plants and important industries because they would not risk losing them to us by marriage in case we put them in the family way. Should this happen and we failed to marry them and take them away with us, they would not for any reason be happy to have a population of half German and half African raised on German soil." In 1964, another Nigerian student in East Germany, Raphael Omenye, recalled the virulent racism displayed by even communist elements of the East German population. Omenye was accosted by some East German civilians who asked him the following questions: *"'Was machen Sie hier, Nigger? Warum bleiben Sie nicht in Ihrem Land, Nigger?' which means 'What are you doing here nigger?' 'Why not remain in your country you nigger?'"* Omenye was then brutally beaten and stabbed and left for dead. This attack was covered up by the East German authorities.[237]

Since the inception of both the German Democratic and Federal Republics in 1949, elements of the conservative CDU/CSU and FDP supported economic links with East Berlin and Moscow. Support for trade with East Germany stemmed from a sentimental desire for an eventual reunification of the two Germanys based on *"peaceful"* trade, greed, and the consolidation of new markets. It is open to question as to whether West German bankers and industrialists would have cooperated with the occupying forces of the USSR and East Germany. It was not unusual for industrialists and other capitalists to cooperate with communist dictatorships during various phases of Red rule. Examples of this phenomenon occurred in the early years of Red China, Sandinista-ruled Nicaragua, Afghanistan under the occupation of the Soviets and their puppet communists, and some of the Soviet satellites in Eastern Europe. However, it was quite clear that powerful West German industrialists and bankers provided the money and technology which enhanced East German and Soviet power. In addition, the Soviets and East Germans used the greed, globalism, and the sentimental nationalism of the West German business community to gain political entry into even anti-communist and conservative circles. Both powerful West German industrialists and East German SED leaders provided stalwart support for Inter-German trade. These views were voiced early in the days of a divided Germany. In the summer of 1950 Walter Ulbricht noted that *"We are sure West German businessmen will sensibly seek to benefit from foreign trade opportunities developed by our efforts."*[238]

Braunthal noted that *"ironically, it is largely the very employers--many of them from the Ruhr and Rhine areas--who have been trading with the Eastern Zone who are also helping to shore up the economy of West Berlin."* Mega-industrialist Alfried Krupp remarked that *"his firm*

---

[237] Gilbert Ofodile. I Shall Never Return: Eight Months in Communist Germany, A Nigerian Student of Journalism Reports (Bechtle Verlag, 1967) page 60.
[238] Joesten, Joachim. "Red China Trade" Barron's National Business and Financial Weekly July 9, 1951 page 9.

was interested in trade with the East bloc countries, and there was no reason why West Germany could not trade with them if other Western states could."[239]

It is also apparent that a succession of all West German governments sought to ignore the underground, illegal trade between the business community and the ruling communists in East Berlin. A CIA document dated from March 1950 noted "**_Federal authorities in West Germany display little desire to cooperate in halting this extra-legal trade, which is already larger than that legally authorized, and border controls are inadequate_**. *Meanwhile, West German industrialists apparently believe not only that extensive trade relations can be developed with the Soviet orbit, including China, but that West Germany cannot exist without this trade…Other effects of this illegal trade will be to contribute to the fulfillment of the East German Two-Year Plan and to the war potential of the Soviet orbit generally; accelerate the attainment by East Germany of economic independence of the West by Western exports of much-needed capital goods; improve gradually the living standards of the East Germans, who will then be less inclined to resist the Communist regime; divert capital goods that could be used in the West; provide propaganda material for German unification to the National Front in East Germany and to ultra-nationalists in West Germany, many of whom favor a modus vivendi with the USSR."*[240]

SPD Bundestag member Herbert Wehner reported in 1951 that West German industrialists legally and illegally shipped $238 million worth of machine tools, ball bearings, steel, and other strategic materials to the East Germans through third countries and dummy firms in Western European countries (Belgium, France, Sweden, and the Netherlands) and West Berlin. It was significant that the CDU-CSU[241] Minister of Economic Affairs Ludwig Erhard downplayed the magnitude of this trade with East Germany. It was reported that these firms also dealt directly with East German companies which acted as fronts for Soviet purchasing agencies.[242]

Early on, various West German business and governmental interests also formed quasi-lobbying agencies to promote trade with East Germany and other communist countries. In 1952, West German bankers and industrialists formed, with the Adenauer government's encouragement, the East Committee to promote trade with the Soviet Union and other communist countries. Executives from Demag, Farbwerke, Hoechst (formerly IG Farben), C.S. Corrsen & Company, and Suedeutsche Bank comprised the board of the East Committee.[243] Also, an Inter-Zonal Trade Office was located in West Berlin and was headed by a West German civil servant, while West German businessmen dealt with East German official import-export firms.[244] Furthermore, the Chairman of the Committee on the East was a close friend of

---

[239] Braunthal, Gerard. The Federation of German Industry in Politics (Cornell University Press, 1965) pages 305-316.

[240] Central Intelligence Agency. "Intelligence Memorandum Number 282: Trade Between East and West Germany" March 28, 1950 Accessed From: http://www.foia.cia.gov/sites/default/files/document_conversions/89801/DOC_0001117633.pdf

[241] Conservative coalition of the Christian Democratic Union and Christian Social Union of West Germany.

[242] "German Goods Aid Soviet in Arming" New York Times April 14, 1951 page 6.

[243] Handler, M.S. "Bonn Unit to Seek Soviet Bloc Trade" New York Times December 19, 1982 page 5.

[244] Gruson, Sydney. "Bonn Pankow Ties are Tenuous" New York Times October 9, 1960 page A4.

Economics Minister Erhard.[245] Braunthal wrote that *"ironically, it is largely the very employers--many of them from the Ruhr and Rhine areas--who have been trading with the Eastern Zone who are also helping to shore up the economy of West Berlin."* Alfried Krupp remarked that *"his firm was interested in trade with the East bloc countries, and there was no reason why West Germany could not trade with them if other Western states could."*[246]

In October 1958, the Minister of Finance, Dr. Fritz Schaeffer conducted top secret political and economic talks with high officials of the East German regime as far back as 1956. These meetings were approved by Chancellor Adenauer. Tetens believed that *"The popular Western view of the Bonn Republic as a bulwark against Communism is a dangerous illusion, nourished by German propaganda. No German statesman or government would hesitate for a moment to strike a bargain with Moscow if the Kremlin were willing to make an attractive offer, such as the return of the lost provinces or a new partition of Poland."*[247] In 1960, one West German businessman concisely summed up the trade policy of the Bonn government with East Germany: *"Business is business and politics is politics."*[248]

West German supporters and apologists viewed the disbursement of *"swing"* credits to East Germany as a means of providing coveted goods and connections to the citizens in that communist country. The *"swing"* credit originally dated back to the 1949 Frankfurt Agreement on Interzonal Trade between West Germany and East Germany. As originally conceived, the *"swing"* credit was an interest free account established between the West German Federal Bank and the East German State Bank to finance temporary imbalances in the level of trade between the two parts of Germany. In practice the *"swing"* has developed into an interest free foreign trade credit for East Germany.[249] It was also seen as a tool to tie East Germany to the Bonn government through economic leverage. The credits were also seen as a humanitarian policy extended to the East Germans. Chancellor Ludwig Erhard summarized the *"swing"* credits as being *"not business, rather it is more significantly a means of maintaining a living connection to the people over there."*[250] Chancellor Erhard viewed the swing credits to East Germany as *"not business, rather it is more significantly a means of maintaining a living connection to the people over there."* An internal Stasi report on the *"the opinion of West German government circles about the further development of trade between the GDR and the FRG"* stated *"of primary importance to the FRG is neither the problem of terms of payment but rather that there be established via trade significant factors for deepening contacts between the GDR and the FRG."*[251]

---

[245] Braunthal, Gerard. The Federation of German Industry in Politics (Cornell University Press, 1965) pages 305-316.
[246] Ibid.
[247] Tetens, T.H. The New Germany and the Old Nazis (Random House 1961) Accessed From: http://spitfirelist.com/books/the-new-germany-and-the-old-nazis/
[248] Gruson, Sydney. "Bonn Pankow Ties are Tenuous" New York Times October 9, 1960 page A4.
[249] Asmus, Ronald D. "New Inter-German Agreement on Swing Credit Announced" Radio Free Europe Research RAD Background Report/141 June 28, 1982 Accessed From: http://files.osa.ceu.hu/holdings/300/8/3/text/26-12-74.shtml
[250] Sarotte, M.E. Dealing with the Devil (University of North Carolina Press, 2001) page 151.
[251] Ibid.

Even in its last days, the SED viewed the *"swing"* credits and other Western grants and loans as a key pillar in ensuring the viability of the state. A secret East German dossier dating October 27, 1989 noted that the GDR needed more capitalist money to bail out their failing communist economy: *"The secret dossier concluded that the realistic alternative for the GDR was 'closer cooperation' with the Federal Republic of Germany 'and other capitalist countries such as France, Austria and Japan who were interested in the GDR as a political counterweight to West Germany.'"*[252]

Apparently, members of the West German public frowned upon the officially-endorsed trade with East Germany. RIAS, the American broadcasting station that operated from West Berlin, received over 800 letters per month from Germans who opposed Bonn's trade credits to East Germany. Robert Lochner, the director of RIAS, noted that the general tone of the letters were *"Will the Federal Republic be so foolish as to help this gangster when he is at the end of his rope?"*[253]

In 1983, executives in various SED front companies assisted East Germany's acquisition of the DM 1 billion loan from West German banks. The Bavarian meat packing firm owned by the Marz brothers purchased large amounts of East German meat. The Marz brothers were close friends of the conservative CDU-CSU politician Franz-Josef Strauss. East Germany used the Marz brothers' influence with Strauss to convince West German banks to loan East Germany DM 1 billion.[254]

The East Germans also procured loans from Western banks with the assistance of conservative politicians in West Germany. In 1983 and 1984, the Stasi officer Alexander Schalck-Golodkowski arranged two loans amounting to 1 billion DM and 950 million for East Germany. These loans were arranged by the SED with the assistance of CSU leader Franz Josef Strauss and were channeled via Western banks.[255]

Along with the far-left and détente-minded elements of the SPD, various powerful conservative politicians supported increased trade relations and the disbursement of credits to East Germany in the 1980s. SPD Bundestag member Andreas von Buelow described former CDU/CSU parliamentarian Hans Josef Strauss as *"an important spy for the German Democratic Republic."* Strauss was accused of providing information to Stasi General and KoKo head Alexander Schlack-Golodkowski. Strauss allegedly sought increased East German orders for West German firms. The information allegedly provided by Strauss was immediately channeled to Stasi General Erich Mielke.[256] Franz Josef Strauss divulged secrets from the CIA, BND, and West German ministries to Stasi General Schalck-Golodkowski. Information that was allegedly provided by Stauss to the Stasi included intelligence on Cruise and Pershing missile sites.

Sometimes East Germany played one West German capitalist off another in pursuit of the most favorable business deal. This was rooted in Lenin's theory of fostering contradictions in the Western capitalist classes as a means of deriving maximum economic and political benefit for

---

[252] Bojunga, Harold. "East German Economy was a Spent Force by Autumn 1989, Dossier Shows" <u>Deutsche Presse-Agentur</u> November 4, 1994

[253] Chamberlin, William. <u>The German Phoenix</u> (Duell, Sloan & Pearce, 1963) page 170.

[254] Colitt, Leslie. <u>Spymaster: The Real-Life Karla, His Moles, and the East German Secret Police</u> (Addison-Wesley Pub., 1995) pages 110-115.

[255] Dale, Gareth. <u>Between State Capitalism and Globalization</u> (Peter Lang, 2004) page 204.

[256] "Socialists charge Franz Josef Strauss spyed for East Germany" <u>Agence France Presse</u> September 1, 1991

the Soviet state. One example of this was a battle of the meat packing firms in West Germany. East Germany initially favored a cattle dealer with SPD connections. At that time, Marz's business then faced potential ruin. Marz's business was re-invigorated through a meeting between his political ally and friend Franz-Josef Strauss and Stasi General Schalck-Golodkowski. In the mid-1980s, exports to East Germany slumped and Marz demanded an increase in meat shipments to East Germany. Marz was able to secure these increased meat exports to East Germany. When the state-owned East German Interflug airline desired to lease Airbus jets, Strauss, who sat on Airbus' Board of Directors, used his political influence to clear COCOM restrictions. Strauss also pressured Mittag and Schalck-Golodkowski to ink contracts with the West German firms MAN and BMD for trade in goods.[257]

The West German intelligence service (BND) reported that the CDU received East German funds in November 1989 and thereafter. This money was part of a 150 million pound fund that was transferred from East Germany to Hungarian banks in November 1989. The CDU maintained close links with the "*reformist*" elements of the Hungarian Socialist Workers' (communist) Party in the late 1980s and during the year 1990. Throughout the 1980s, East German Commercial Coordination (KoKo) officials, top CDU/CSU official Franz-Josef Strauss, and the Marz brothers all hunted together in communist Hungary. They also enjoyed gambling at the casino at the Hilton Hotel in Budapest. Marz was involved in a scheme to fund the CSU from West German government subsidies initially provided to companies which conducted business in communist Hungary. Perhaps this funding was at least a partial impetus for the CDU/CSU government to provide increased credits and outright economic privileges to the East German regime in the late 1980s and early 1990. It should also be added that the SED laundered money in the USSR and Ceausescu's Romania in November 1989.[258]

Volkswagen President Carl Hahn noted to the East German Minister for Foreign Trade Gerhard Beil that his company wanted to shift production from West to East Germany. Hahn reasoned that West Germany was "*not stable enough*" and because of "*the rising costs in FRG[259] industry.*" In 1984, the East German firm IFA and Volkswagen set up a joint venture factory in East Germany. The engines were sold outside East Germany while others were installed in East German Wartburg cars. The director of West German firm Salzgitter insisted to East German Foreign Trade Minister Beil that "*Salzgitter needs the trade with the socialist countries.*" Wilhelm Scheider, chairperson of Krupps, noted to Minister Beil that the West German steel industry was in a poor state and that "*the consequence in a free market economy would be bankruptcy.*" In classified documents, the head of the Ruhr-based firm Gute-Hoffnungshutte (code-named in Stasi documents "*Lodz*") noted to Beil that his firm, along with a consortium of West German companies indicated a desire to build a nuclear power plant in East Germany. "*Lodz*" gave three reasons for consummating the nuclear power plant deal: the "*most important*" was that "*the FRG government and industry are seeking to build a counterweight to the anti-nuclear movement;*" there were "*gigantic stockpiles of valuable nuclear power equipment which it would like to reduce;*" and "*East Germany has a clear nuclear power strategy and no*

---

[257] Dale, Gareth. Between State Capitalism and Globalization (Peter Lang, 2004) pages 228-232.
[258] Grey, Stephen and Goetz, John. "Communists linked to Kohl fund" The Sunday Times (United Kingdom) May 7, 2000
[259] FRG was the acronym of the Federal Republic of Germany, which better known as West Germany.

problems with its population." In other words, West German business considered the controlled and cowed East German populace and workforce an asset to enhancing their profits.[260]

Erich Honecker argued before the Soviet Politburo his belief that East and West Germany entered into a *"coalition of reason"* where the East Germans held an upper hand in influencing West Germany. Businessman Walther Leisler-Kiep recalled that *"even the big time capitalists in West Germany were so greatly interested in pursuing their business deals that they supported improved relations with East Germany."* Honecker noted to his Soviet Politburo colleagues that Kiep, who was a major stockholder in Hoescht AG and member of the presidium and treasurer of the CDU, was a long time booster of tighter East-West relations. At a lavish dinner party at the Krupp Villa Hugel in Essen, Kiep noted that he marveled *"at the strange symbolism of seeing Honecker mingle with his 'class enemies' in the obscenely ostentatious main hall of the Krupp family's erstwhile residence."* Honecker asked Kiep about his visit to the Krupp party in Essen. Kiep responded: *"What do you think would be happening here if we had an SPD government in Bonn-most of us would be standing outside demonstrating against you."* Honecker reportedly laughed and stated *"I can well imagine that."*[261]

The West Germans were well aware that their aid and trade bolstered the life of the communist regime in East Berlin. One West German official noted in 1989 that Bonn's aid was *"subsidizing Stalinism"* in East Germany.[262] Jonathan Zaitlan also concluded that *"What saved the GDR from defaulting was West German capitalism. In perhaps the ironic twist in the GDR's history the staunchly anti-communist center-right coalition in West Germany rescued Honecker and Mittag from the consequences of their bungling. In fact, the Kohl government proved even more generous than its Social Democratic predecessors."*[263] The chief statistician for East Germany, Arno Donda reflected on how West German credits and loans eased East Berlin's financial crisis of 1982: *"It was quite clear on the basis of all the material known to me at the time…that we were headed for economic collapse. But the so-called Strauss credit and the following agreements…managed to allay these fears to a considerable extent."* One historian noted that the East German *"socialists could always count on the help of capitalists who placed profit margins above appeals to national security."*[264]

The East German SED leadership and its propagandists launched a campaign which sought to entice further free trade between East and West Germany. Internationalist and even libertarian-free market sounding rhetoric was opportunistically employed to entice industrialists and politicians to take the free trade bait dangled by the SED. Big business was also seen as part of the SED and CPSU support network in West Germany. In 1987, the SED economics boss Guenter Mittag praised industrialists from the Saar (West Germany) for their *"effective and decisive contribution made by industrial circles to improve the climate of co-operation between the two German states."*[265] Even the slogans at the Leipzig Trade Fairs promoted free trade

---

[260] Dale, Gareth. Between State Capitalism and Globalization (Peter Lang, 2004) pages 219-228.
[261] Kiep, Walther Leisler. Bridge Builder: An Insider's Account of Over Sixty Years in Post-War (Purdue University Press, 2012) pages 113-120.
[262] McCartney, Robert J. "West German Aid Helps East Germany Avoid Crisis" Washington Post August 8, 1989 page A14.
[263] Zatlin, Jonathan. The Currency of Socialism (Cambridge University Press 2007) page 140.
[264] Ibid, page 184.
[265] "Guenter Mittag and Gerhard Beil meet Saarland industrialists" East German Press Agency September 12, 1987

between the East and West. The September 1989 Leipzig Trade Fair opened in East Germany under the slogan *"For open-door trading and technological progress."*[266]

The East Germans launched an aggressive propaganda against embargoes. In September 1987, Mittag noted that *"Embargo measures harm overall international trade relations…We must understand that they have an effect everywhere."*[267] In a conversation with Mittag, West German industrialist Otto Wolff noted in 1984 that: *"…embargoes and protectionism are futile ways of exerting political pressure. The history of trade has shown that such practices have always harmed their authors. Otto Wolff called for the extension of trade and economic relations with the socialist countries and emphasized the multi-faceted export and import relations with the GDR in which small and medium enterprises are playing an increasing part."*[268]

Mittag noted that *"the GDR advocated free world trade. Mutually advantageous trade had a firm place in our trade with the capitalist states. It was part of our policy of peaceful co-existence. In the interests of the continuation of what had already been achieved in the process of detente in Europe great importance was ascribed to trade relations. At the same time this served the safeguarding of peace. When touring the Fair Guenter Mittag said that, as far as the capitalist countries' relations with the socialist countries in the sense of peaceful coexistence were concerned, all attempts to differentiate between individual socialist countries were useless."*[269] In 1987, Erich Honecker asserted his opposition to economic nationalism as carried out by the West when he remarked that: *"dangerous manifestations of protectionism, attempts at building barriers against competition and other obstacles to trade are making themselves noticeable. At the same time, our trade relations with the capitalist countries are part of our total dynamic economic development. We want to derive benefit for this through the purchase of raw materials and above all of equipment and plant."*[270] Mittag stated to an audience of industrialists in 1987 that: *"I am not betraying any secrets when I tell you the following: The GDR's scientific and industrial potential, which continually gains strength from a highly developed education system, puts us into the position of transcending embargoes. Sometimes this happens more quickly than some people may have believed possible. International trade relations alone suffer damage from embargo measures. This should be recognized everywhere."*[271]

Another motivation for the collaboration of West German industrialists with the SED was protection from the class-based reprisals of invading Soviet and East German invasion forces. Evidence of this existed as far back as the late 1940s. Two types of West German businessman existed in the Federal Republic since the late 1940s: the Inter-Zonal trader and the so-called *reinsurer* or *Ruckversicherer* who traded with the Soviet Zone (SBZ). The *Ruckversicherer*, as he was contemptuously known by West Germans, was a businessman who funded the communists and/or extreme nationalist organizations which maintained strong ties to the Soviets

---

[266] "The 1989 Leipzig Autumn Fair" East German News Agency September 28, 1989
[267] Jautz, Kenneth. "Honecker Deputy Criticizes Trade Embargoes" The Associated Press September 9, 1987
[268] "Guenter Mittag at Hanover Trade Fair" East German News Agency April 7, 1984
[269] "GDR-FRG Relations: Mittag in Bonn and Hanover" East German News Agency April 18, 1980
[270] "Meeting with Businessmen in Cologne" East German News Agency September 11, 1987
[271] "Meeting with Businessmen in Cologne" ADN September 11, 1987

and East Germans. The *Ruckversicherer* financed these elements as a means of ensuring exemption from arrest or execution in the event of a Soviet occupation of West Germany.[272]

This was confirmed by journalists and intelligence sources. The U. S. High Commissioner for Bavaria George Shuster reported in 1951 that the *"Ruhr industrialists were taking out insurance with the Communist party and that the coffers of the Communist party were filled with their money."*[273]

Habe noted that *"The Ruhr industrialists are neither dreamers nor particularly patriotic. At the moment their predominant aim is to earn as many dollars as fast as possible. But, more important, they prefer to work as our suppliers or employees rather than as our allies. In case of Russian occupation they would like to be able to point out that they have just done a 'job' without active political support of the West. There is hardly a day when Allied Intelligence agencies do not find out that war material is being shipped from the Ruhr to the East, and at the Moscow Trade Conference in April 1952, German industry was represented by an impressive delegation, led by Ludwig Krumm, West Germany's No. 1 leather manufacturer who returned with an order for shoes amounting to eighteen million marks. This does not mean that the leaders of German industry and the masters of the Ruhr are pro-Communist or pro-Russian. It does mean, however, that they are perfectly aware of the Russian menace and that they prefer to maintain the greatest possible neutrality. To serve us as blacksmiths is good business, involving a minimum of risk. To furnish us in the name of Western solidarity does not mean more dollars but only increases the chances to be taken."*[274]

In other words, the biggest West German capitalists paid protection money to the communists. The industrialists thought that such protection money would buy them their lives from the execution squads of the East Germans and their West German communist allies. This was a similar path that elements of German big business took when they helped fund the National Socialists in the 1920s and early 1930s. However, the protection money proved meaningless when the Nazis imposed severe controls over the private economy in Germany and even jailed and executed businessmen for various *"crimes."* Without question, the Soviets and East Germans would have eliminated the West German big business elites once their economic usefulness was used up.

Fast forward to the 1970s and 1980s and the protection payments continued. Twenty-one foreign firms, such as Japan's Nissho Iwai Corporation and West Germany's Salamander shoes, donated a total of 631,450 marks in 1976 to the West German Communist Party (DKP). This was done at the request of the East German government. Fourteen of the firms that donated money to the DKP were from West Germany, while the remaining were Swiss, Danish, Dutch and American companies. The donated funds were intended for supporting the convention of the West German communist party and parliamentary elections in 1976.[275]

Sometimes West German big business paid money to the SED for lucrative investment opportunities in East Germany. It was reported that AEG remitted payments of 300,000 DM to the East German government in 1984. This was essentially bribe money extorted by the East

---

[272] Tauber, Kurt P. Beyond Eagle and Swastika (Wesleyan University Press, 1967)

[273] Pearson, Drew. "Germans Cutting Throats by Help to Red Nations" Charleston Gazette March 19, 1951 page 6.

[274] Habe, Hans. Our Love Affair with Germany (Putnam, 1953) page 148.

[275] "Foreign firms donated to West German communist party in 1976: report" Agence France Presse October 21, 1993

Germans for companies to maintain lucrative contracts with the ruling SED. It was revealed that Western firms were extorted to the tune of seven million Deutschemarks in the late 1980s.[276]

A valuable tool for the Soviets and the SED in luring Western businessmen to trade with the communists was the Leipzig Trade Fair. Previously, the Nazis used the Fair as a tool to lure Western capitalists, Soviet trade officials, and fellow fascist states and puppet governments to trade with Hitler. Under East German stewardship, known German industrialists who produced war material for the National Socialists and colluded with Hitler in perpetrating war crimes were opportunistically whitewashed at the Leipzig Fair in an effort to gain valuable technology and other types of goods. Big business was viewed as the link between the East German leadership and the West German conservative parties, such as the CDU-CSU-FDP coalition. HVA Chief General Markus Wolf recalled that *"We started using the Leipzig trade fair to make contacts with the business community and through them conservative politicians and public figures who believed that by cooperating with the East they were somehow ensuring there would be no full rupture between the two halves of Germany."* Businessmen reportedly did not mind Wolf's status as a Stasi General; Wholesale steel trader Christian Steinrucke was not bothered by Wolf's status as a Stasi general and they *"got on famously."*[277] The CD-CSU-FDP coalition became a stalwart supporter of increased economic engagement with East Germany and the Soviet Union.

Alfried Krupp, visited the Leipzig Trade Fair (1959) in East Germany and met with Foreign Trade Minister Heinrich Rau. Krupp was welcomed with open arms. The communists were so eager to import goods from Krupp that they actually adjusted their propaganda which shifted more of the blame for Nazi war production to IG Farben and the electro-technical industries.[278]

During the Leipzig Trade Fair in 1959, Khrushchev was present, along with executives of Krupp, Phonix-Rheinrohr, Mannesmann, and Klockner-Humboldt. Soviet Deputy Foreign Minister Zorin, the commander of the Group of Soviet Forces Germany, General Sakharov, and the Soviet Ambassador to East Germany Pervukhin were also present at the Leipzig Trade Fair of 1959. SED signs emblazoned with the slogans Krupp *"War Criminal"* and *"Arch-Imperialist Krupp"* were taken down by the East Germans during the Leipzig Trade Fair.[279]

An East German history of the Krupps noted that *"The principal German war criminals were I.G. Farben and the Nazi electronics industry. Krupp, by comparison, played a very minor role in war production."* Khrushchev noted at the Leipzig Trade Fair of 1959 that *"Tell Herr Krupp that he is the kind of capitalist we Communists can do business with… We intend a long association with him."*[280]

In 1969, executives of the much-maligned West German companies such as AEG and Siemens were waved quickly and politely through communist border guard checkpoints on the Inter-German border. These delegations were on their way to the Leipzig Trade Fair. In 1969, an

---

[276] "AEG Admits to Paying Large Sums in Response to East German Extortion" Guardian April 7, 1994 page 16.
[277] Wolf, Markus and McElvoy, Anne. Man Without a Face (PublicAffairs, 1999) page 78.
[278] "East German Welcome to Herr Krupp" Times of London March 4, 1959 page 9.
[279] Sedar, Irving and Greenberg, Harold J. Behind the Egyptian Sphinx (Chilton Company 1960) Accessed From:
http://www.archive.org/stream/behindtheegyptia007284mbp/behindtheegyptia007284mbp_djvu.txt
[280] "Krupp Finds Red Trade Boobytrap" Galveston News October 8, 1959 page 8.

East German Foreign Ministry official commented that the West German companies that were formerly accused of war profiteering and crimes also produced *"things for peaceful purposes."*[281]

The Interhotel[282] chains in East Germany became a tool in the arsenal of the Stasi to compromise many VIP visitors, such as diplomats, businessmen, and politicians. A Stasi document noted *"Sex and alcohol prove potent weapons in the war to defend socialism. It is an important segment in the defense of the state."*[283] Sex and alcohol were plentiful at the Interhotels. Former Stasi operative Clara Schneider noted *"...basically anyone that we thought could be of use in putting the DDR case abroad and of influencing policy in capitalist countries we viewed as essentially hostile."* She was asked to become a prostitute agent tasked with the entrapment and blackmail of foreign VIPs. She was shocked at the decadent means and tools used to recruit such high level Western visitors. Schneider recalled that: *"I was an ardent communist but not very good looking. One day this gorgeous hunk came by as I was leaving the school in Dresden where I taught and said he wanted to talk to me about government business. He asked if I would be interested in serving my country. Before I knew it I was in a room with three other girls being shown assorted lingerie and different perfumes. It shocked my morality - I thought they wanted us to become prostitutes. They said it was for the good of the Fatherland and world peace."*[284] The East Germans were depraved enough to deploy even underage prostitute agents to entrap Western businessmen and diplomats. Male prostitutes as young as 12 years old were utilized by the Stasi to entrap Western diplomats and businessmen visiting East Germany. Each year, 2,000 Stasi prostitutes arrived at the the Leipzig trade fair on so-called *"whores trains"* to target foreign businessmen and government officials who possessed valuable hard currency and intelligence information.[285] Western businessmen were entrapped by prostitutes who were registered with the police or involved with espionage for the Stasi. Such prostitutes were active at the Palasthotel and Metropole Hotel. Many Western businessmen and professionals were targeted by these Stasi prostitutes since many of these visitors were involved in financial deals with East German government-owned firms.[286]

Early on, East German hotels were closely monitored by the Stasi, while personnel were ordered to don *"friendly faces"* when processing clients amongst visiting Westerners. As of August 1954, listening devices were installed in the Leipzig HO Hotel Bayrischer Hof by the Stasi. This hotel had special rooms where the Stasi could eavesdrop on conversations by the hotel guests. The hotel was reserved for mainly journalists, especially from capitalist countries. Employees at the hotel were screened by the Stasi and unreliable personnel were dismissed and replaced. The hotel manager named Kummer was closely tied with the Stasi. He took over the

---

[281] Blumenthal, Ralph. "Leipzig Hospitality Cited" <u>New York Times</u> March 13, 1969 page 10.

[282] The Interhotels were an East German corporation which controlled all of the luxury hotels geared towards foreigners. It was formed in 1965 and were closely monitored by the Stasi.

[283] Hall, Allan. "Stasi Files Reveal Hot Stuff From the Cold War" <u>The Scotsman</u> March 12, 2002 page 10.

[284] Hall, Allen. "Stasi Files Show Full Extent of Cruel Reign" <u>Scotland on Sunday</u> September 26, 1999 page 22.

[285] Staunton, Dennis. "Stasi used boy prostitutes to trap Western diplomats" <u>The Observer</u> April 5, 1998 page 6.

[286] Smith, Duncan. <u>Walls and Mirrors</u> (University Press of America, 1988) pages 101-103.

Bayrischer Hof and was said to be a *"man of excellent manners."*[287] Hill reported in 1982 that *"those East Germans who have contact with Westerners through their jobs in international hotels appear to have undergone special training. They are efficient, exceedingly polite but rather stiff..."*[288]

One East German noted that the Interhotel bureaucracy dressed Western, bought Western, drove Western cars, traveled to Western countries, all with the intent of drawing Western tourists.[289] The Western-built, luxury hotels in East Germany became egregious symbols of the corruption of the SED elite and its collusion with Western big business. In December 1989, the newspaper Der Morgen reported on the SED's *"gala programs at the Grand Hotel and other facilities in East Berlin, entrance to which was denied to average citizens; it described costly shows and opulent candlelight dinners on offer for DM 500 or more. There, party members with hard currency to burn rubbed elbows with Western high society. It was a dreadful spectacle."*[290]

In 1987, the Japanese company Kojima built the East Berlin Grand Hotel, which was listed by the Leading Hotels Association as one of the 200 best hotels in the world in 1988. It provided chauffeured Mercedes Benz limousine service and other luxury amenities.[291] Copies of Western newspapers and periodicals were sold to the mostly foreign clientele from the capitalist world who were lodged at the Grand Hotel.[292] The Grand Hotel's East German Deputy Director noted *"We built this hotel to be able to offer a good product on the international market. We operate on the old capitalist principle that when the customer is happy, he buys more."*[293]

The Metropol, Palasthotel, Grand, Merkur, and Bellevue were among the most luxurious of the East German Interhotels. Several were the object of praise from VIPs who were lodged in them. Visiting Austrian businesswoman Astrid Hausmann noted: *"It's simply marvelous. The staff is helpful, friendly, everything quiet, luxurious, it's one of the best hotels I know, east or west."*[294] In 1988, Takeo Shinde, a spokesman for the Bank of Tokyo noted this about the Metropol Hotel and the East German border troops: *"The (East German) border soldiers even greet me because they recognize me now…I feel very comfortable there. The employees are very well-trained and very helpful."* Alan F. Delp, a senior vice president of the First National Bank of Chicago, noted *"The pleasant surprise has been that it is so easy to go back and forth. Very honestly, it couldn't be easier."* Jay Newman, senior vice president with Shearson Lehman

---

[287] SSD Spies on Visitors to Leipzig Fair Radio Free Europe Research Eastern Europe September 24, 1954 Accessed From: http://www.osaarchivum.org/greenfield/repository/osa:9adc3ce1-fc40-489b-8a34-d37ea045b192

[288] Hill, Sandra. "Letter from East Berlin: Prussian tradition and Soviet discipline" United Press International January 4, 1982

[289] Gleye, Paul. Behind the Wall (SIU Press, 1991) page 136.

[290] Keithly, David M. The Collapse of East German Communism (Praeger, 1992) pages 198-204.

[291] Williams, Carol J. "Capitalist splendor marks East Berlin hotel" The Financial Post May 30, 1989 page 14.

[292] Echikson, William. "Elegance is 'In' in Eastern Europe" Christian Science Monitor March 9, 1989 page 6.

[293] Williams, Carol J. "Capitalist splendor marks East Berlin hotel" The Financial Post May 30, 1989 page 14.

[294] Echikson, William. "Elegance is 'In' in Eastern Europe" Christian Science Monitor March 9, 1989 page 6.

International, a financial services firm, called East Berlin's Grand Hotel *"the best hotel in the world."*[295]

Even during the 1950s, the East German trade mission directors cooperated with foreign businessmen in the Leipzig Fairs. They also assumed the mannerisms and airs of the Western capitalists. They frequented luxury hotels such as the Astoria, had access to fine liquors, foods such as caviar and roasted meats, and having fun at the Postkutsche night club.[296]

It also appeared that important elements of the West German big business and conservative leadership were drawn to the concept of increased East-West German relations through a shared admiration for what was perceived as a socially conservative and authoritarian communism and an internationalist attitude which had forsaken any notions of the West German national interest and the NATO alliance. As previously mentioned, the East Committee was formed within the West German Employers' Federation (BDI) in 1952. Otto Wolff von Amerongen was a leading force in the Committee in promoting increased trade between the Soviet bloc and West Germany. The motto of Wolff's firm Otto Wolff AG was *"our job is not to rescue the Fatherland but to do business."* SED economic boss Gunter Mittag was viewed *"by many top managers in the West as absolutely one of their own."* Jurgen Nitz noted that he always heard *"exceptionally positive opinions towards the East German leaders…above all from the top people in the West German business community"* as well as from CDU leaders such as Leisler-Kiep. Schalck-Golodkowski was "a *favorite conversation partner amongst members of the West German political establishment of all stripes"* which included Theo Waigel of the CSU, Wolfgang Schauble of the CDU, and Count Lambsdorff of the Free Democrats (FDP). In 1988, Berthold Beitz of Krupps wrote a letter to Mittag which indicated that he was *"overwhelmed by the beautiful presents"* he had received from the East German state. Beitz bragged of his *"great pleasure"* of hunting with the SED leaders and of his desire *"to have a GDR artist paint my portrait."* According to East German officials, Otto Wolff admired the Prussian aspects of East Germany. Wolff was a member of the Bilderberg Group and the Trilateral Commission, which were two powerful globalist organizations populated by international elitists. Wolff noted in a communication to Mittag in 1987 that: *"My very worthy dear Mr. Mittag: You once told me that, should I ever deem it appropriate I could contact you outside of our official roles if something arose pertaining to affairs of my company."* Wolff heard that an East German steel making firm invited outside firms to participate in a major investment project. Mittag was requested to intervene on behalf of Wolff's firm. Mittag assented to Wolff's request.[297]

CDU/CSU politician Franz-Josef Strauss admired East Germany's Prussian authoritarianism and reactionary family policy. Strauss also praised East Germany's repression of three evils that he hated: *"hashish, pornography and…long hair."* Strauss found his worldview similar to Honecker, as opposed to East Germany's *"long haired"* dissidents. Strauss phoned Honecker to express his contempt for the *"crazy"* East German Stepan Krawczyk and his fellow dissident *"dreamers."* East German journalists who opposed Strauss were taken to task by their SED superiors.[298]

---

[295] Petty, Terrence. "Communist East Berlin Opens Up For Capitalists From World Bank Talks" <u>Associated Press</u> September 28, 1988

[296] Gilroy, Harry. "Leipzig Develops Capitalist Habit" <u>New York Times</u> September 12, 1958 page 5.

[297] Dale, Gareth. <u>Between State Capitalism and Globalization</u> (Peter Lang, 2004) pages 219-228.

[298] Ibid, pages 228-232.

Wolff reported in 1981 that he *"emphasized"* to an East German official *"that the West German business community due to its interests would practice restraint and not intervene in the internal affairs of the People's Republic of Poland."* Joseph Marz sympathized with East German authorities for their refusal to issue visas for *"Greens and other politicians from the Left scene."* Marz expressed his hope that East German dissidents would not emigrate to West Germany, for *"we already have enough of those Bahros, Biermanns, Krawczyks, and Kliers in West Germany."* FDP leader Count Lambsdorff expressed a lack of sympathy for Krawczyk and urged puppet East German Church leaders to give oppositionists *"a good scolding."* A leading CDU politician, Lothar Spath, sympathized with the East German state in its worsening relations with the church and stated to Schlack-Golodkowski his disdain for East German radical *"clerics who pursue the interests of oppositional forces which otherwise have little to do with the church."*[299]

Even more sinister were the examples of covert communists who posed as respectable conservative or libertarian businessmen in West Germany. While they were not representative of the overall ideology of the business community in West Germany, their existence should certainly not be overlooked. The West German millionaire businessman and Free Democratic Party (FDP)[300] member Hannsheinz Porst was uncovered as a covert agent of the East German Socialist Unity Party (SED-ruling communist party in East Germany) and the Stasi. He was a secret Marxist who posed as a member of libertarian FDP.[301]

Hard currency monetary transactions between companies and individuals in West and East Germany helped fund subversive activities of the KPD/DKP. During the days of the outright Soviet occupation of Eastern Germany, the SED engaged in hard currency business operations that funded subversive activities in West Germany and international terrorist movements. Between 1945 and 1990, the SED employed some of the most versatile communist capitalists to raise revenue for the rulers in East Berlin and Moscow. Keithly observed that *"managers and sales representatives of KoKo companies in the West were often members of the local communist parties, class warriors wielding capitalism's formidable weapons to expedite its demise. To renew their ideological vigor they would be summoned to the GDR at least once a year for indoctrination sessions led by Professor Max Schmidt, director of the Institute for Politics and Economics in East Berlin or the infamous Otto Reinhold, professor at the Central Committee's Academy for the Social Sciences."*[302]

In 1948, it was reported that the Soviet Zone Administration financed the communist party in West Germany through hard currency sales of consumer goods through Rasno Export Corporation outlets.[303] As of June 1, 1953 the Deutsche Notenbank[304] maintained cash reserves of 25 million Deutschmarks. The accounts kept at the Deutsche Notenbank were: Interzonal Trade, Other Payments, and AS-Account. The Other Payments account received Deutschmarks from S-Bahn passengers/traffic, confiscated money at East German-West German border points, and the mandatory currency exchanges for visitors to East Germany. These sources earned 5.6

---

[299] Ibid, pages 231-233.
[300] The Free Democratic Party (FDP) was a libertarian-leaning party in West German and later unified German politics.
[301] "West German Millionaire Marxist Was Red Spy" Stars and Stripes June 1, 1969 page 4.
[302] Keithly, David M. The Collapse of East German Communism (Praeger, 1992) pages 198-204.
[303] "Berlin Reds Seeking Western Currency" New York Times July 2, 1948 page 2.
[304] The Deutsche Notenbank was the state-owned central bank in East Germany.

million Deutschmarks for the East Germans. Deutschmarks from the AS Account was shipped via courier to Czechoslovakia and then to Switzerland and was exchanged for Swiss marks. The excess Deutschmarks were used to fund illegal Interzonal trade and subversive groups in West Germany.[305] Hence, travel, tourism, and trade between the two Germanys were exploited by the SED to subvert the Bonn government.

Even the seemingly innocent sales of consumer goods for hard currency were used to strengthen the international communist allies of the East Germans. Profits and revenues accrued from the sales undertaken by the East German gift export firm GENEX were channeled to so-called "*national liberation movements*" (terrorists) in the Third World.[306] The Kohl government allowed subsidiaries of GENEX to open in Stuttgart and West Berlin.[307] Thus, the actions of the Kohl government helped ensure that East Berlin was in receipt of hard currencies which were then channeled to various leftist terrorist movements. Imported Western technologies were channeled by the East Germans to terrorist movements.

GENEX was first established by the East Germans in 1962 as a mail order gift service. East Germans with relatives in the West could acquire high quality goods as "*gifts*" from their brethren in the West. Between 1975 and 1988, the total profits accrued from sales by GENEX numbered 24 billion DM. GENEX operated from Denmark and Switzerland and serviced customers through those intermediary companies. GENEX even sold Soviet bloc-made cars along with Volkswagen Passats and Golfs, BMWs, Ford Orions, Fiats, and Peugeots to East German customers. The "*conservative*" Kohl government allowed subsidiaries of GENEX to open in Stuttgart and West Berlin.[308]

The Intershops were set up in 1955 in the port cities of Wismar, Rostock, and Stralsund originally to service foreign sailors. The first Intershop that opened in August 1955 in Rostock was successful. More Intershops were opened at East German international airports, border crossing areas, and in Leipzig to service Fair guests. In July 1970, Stasi General Alexander Schalck-Golodkowski, the Minister of Finance, and the Deputy Minister of Finance proposed a plan for "*a rapid increase of hard currency revenues in Intershop trade.*" In 1974, Intershop profits totaled 286 million DM; 829 million DM in 1980; and 1.16 billion DM in the first part of 1989. Initially, the only East Germans that were permitted access to the Intershops were:
1) Employees in the service/tourist sector.
2) High ranking officials who traveled to the West.
3) East German diplomatic personnel.

The number of Intershops grew from 270 in 1970 to 416 in 1986. In 1977, Intershops were built near the dumps in Ketzin and Schoneiche in order to attract the business of West Berlin garbage men.[309]

Despite the socialist inequality rendered by the Intershops and other hard currency operations, the SED leadership viewed them as invaluable to the East German economy. Walter Ulbricht characterized the Intershops in 1965 as "*stopgaps*" and a "*necessary evil.*" Stasi

---

[305] "Western Marks in East Germany" Radio Free Europe Research July 9, 1953 Accessed From: http://www.osaarchivum.org/greenfield/repository/osa:8d3f27de-c7b6-48ce-958a-e0edc7a26342

[306] Colitt, Leslie. "East Germany's leaders face threat of strikes" Financial Times January 15, 1990 page 2.

[307] Zatlin, Jonathan. The Currency of Socialism (Cambridge University Press 2007) page 207.

[308] Ibid, pages 271-274.

[309] Ibid, pages 245-261 and 280-283.

General Alexander Schalck-Golodkowski noted in 1988 that *"revenues from the Intershops have reached such dimensions that we cannot do without this income in the interest of securing the balance of payments."*[310] In 1977, Honecker defended the Intershops by stating *"These shops obviously aren't permanent companions of socialism...But we can't ignore the fact that the rising number of visitors is bringing more such currency among us than before...Naturally, we haven't overlooked the fact that the citizens of the German Democratic Republic who have no such funds are at a disadvantage, in a certain sense, compared to those who have such currency at their disposal...Through the Intershops, we have created the possibility that these funds stay with us in the country...You have to look completely coolly at both sides of the coin."*[311]

The SED corporation Intrac managed East Germany's so-called "*ecological*" waste dumps where Western European firms disposed of industrial byproducts, often toxic, at very reasonable prices. As Keithly wrote: *"'Ecology' in SED Newspeak meant turning large tracts of land into Europe's waste-yard in order to acquire hard currency."*[312] West German, Spanish, Italian and other Western companies hauled chemical and toxic waste to an East German landfill in Schonberg.[313] This netted the East Germans $590 million in hard currency for communist coffers since the mid- 1970s.[314] By January 1990, West Germany and West Berlin shipped 1 million tons of garbage per year to East German dumps in Schoeneiche and Vorketzin.[315]

The SED also fleeced great quantities of cash from the West German government and populace. Compulsory exchanges of Western currency by visiting foreigners traveling to East Germany totaled 360 million DM per year. Transportation payments to East Germany totaled 8.3 million DM between 1972 and 1989. The West Germans agreed to pay East Germany to construct a 2.4 billion DM highway system between Berlin and other cities such as Hamburg. The Bundesbank estimated that East German assets in West Germany totaled 2-3 billion DM. In 1988, the Staatsbank held 300 million DM on the account of the East German government.[316] Two West German firms with majority government ownership Preusen AG and Bewag AG shared the full costs in linking the East German and West German power networks. The West German Federal and Bavarian governments shared the costs with East Germany in the construction of a sewage plant in the East German town of Sonnenberg. Between 1983 and 1985, West Germany spent 68 million DM on three sewage plants in East Berlin. The West Berlin Senate spent 70 million DM on the waste disposal site in Schoneiche. East Germany also paid West Germany 300 million DM each year for West Germany to process East German steel. It was reported that this ruined the West German state-subsidized firm ARBED Saarstahl. The state-owned firms Volkswagen and Salzgitter-Konzern purchased East German steel. Hard currency gas stations in East Germany called Intertank provided the SED with an annual income

---

[310] Ibid.
[311] Miller, Stephen H. "Berlin" <u>The Associated Press</u> October 12, 1977
[312] Keithly, David M. <u>The Collapse of East German Communism</u> (Praeger, 1992) pages 198-204.
[313] Aeppel, Timothy. "West Pays Price for Dumping on East" <u>Christian Science Monitor</u> February 10, 1989 Page 4.
[314] Czuczka, Tony. "Citizen Protest Cuts Lucrative Shipments Of Foreign Waste" <u>Associated Press</u> January 26, 1990
[315] Ibid.
[316] Zatlin, Jonathan. <u>The Currency of Socialism</u> (Cambridge University Press 2007) page 282.

of 100 million DM.[317] In 1988, five hundred bankers were lodged in luxury hotels in East Berlin and added at least $270,000 to the state's coffers.[318]

The East Germans bartered political prisoners for West German cash and goods between 1963 and 1990. Thirty four thousand East German children and prisoners were exchanged for 3.44 billion deutschmarks.[319] In reference to the sale of East German prisoners to the West, Schalck noted *"How did I morally explain it? When someone was educated in the DDR and cost the state 500,000 marks, then it is legitimate, at the very least, to ask when someone left whether taxpayers should bear that cost or whether part could be recovered."*[320] West German SPD official Egon Bahr stated in a conversation with East German negotiator Michael Kohl in 1972 that *"in conjunction with the exit of the children, certain transfer payments probably should be made."*[321]

West Germany also activated trade with the Soviets by the late 1940s. West German business interests were stalwart supporters of such exchanges. They exerted their influence with Chancellor Adenauer's government. In 1949, the foreign press noted that a group of ultraconservative businessmen and diplomats (among them Dr. Herman Puender, banker Hermann Abs, ex-Minister Dr. Andreas Hermes, Professor Ludwig Ehrhard, and ex-Ambassador Count Rudolf Nadolny) discussed the possibilities of Russo-German collaboration. Dr. Adenauer cautioned his CDU/CSU and big business friends to deceptively downplay relations with the Soviets: *"We must move very cautiously. We ought not to give the impression, either in Germany or in the United States, which we shall collaborate in any way with the Russians."*[322]

Christian Kuhlemann (CDU), Chairman of the Bundestag Committee on Foreign Trade, suggested in November 1950 that the Federal Republic establish an Eastern Trade Office (*Osthandelskontor*) to regulate material exchanges with the Soviet bloc. The BDI supported a plan to sponsor a *"fusion of West German interests vis-à-vis the state trading organizations in the East bloc countries"* just *"as soon as the political situation has changed."* The BDI supported a *"useful, real, and constantly developing business relationship"* with the East. This trade relationship required *"centralized steering and advising for business with the USSR, and if necessary also with the satellite states, through a committee based on the cooperation of the sectoral interest groups (Fachverbände)."* The BDI memorandum listed the duties of the new Eastern Committee as *"advising and disseminating information"* on the German side and *"especially by making business connections"* between Germans and Soviets. At the same time, Soviet export agencies began promoting the export of supplies of wood, grain, and oil to West German import firms. Hans Kroll, head of the East-West Trade Group in the Federal Ministry for Economics, understood that the combination of political pressure from the SPD and economic pressure from the business community compelled the government to improve trade relations with

---

[317] Lisiecki, Jerzy. "Financial and Material Transfers between East and West Germany" Soviet Studies July 1990 pages 513-534.
[318] Petty, Terrence. "Communist East Berlin Opens Up For Capitalists From World Bank Talks" Associated Press September 28, 1988
[319] "East Germans Sold Their People to West" Sunday Telegraph December 16, 2007
[320] Tanner, Adam. "It's Alexander the Freight: Life of East German Wheeler-Dealer" Birmingham Post April 29, 2000 page 21.
[321] Sarotte, M.E. Dealing with the Devil (University of North Carolina Press, 2001) page 152.
[322] Tetens, T.H. The New Germany and the Old Nazis (Random House 1961) Accessed From: http://spitfirelist.com/books/the-new-germany-and-the-old-nazis/

the Soviets. In May 1952, the Bundestag resolved unanimously that *"the remaining limits on German freedom of action in the control of merchandise trade and -- so far as is legally possible -- in the conclusion of trade treaties with East bloc countries must be eliminated as soon as possible."*[323] Hans Habe noted that *"The Ruhr industrialists are neither dreamers nor particularly patriotic. At the moment their predominant aim is to earn as many dollars as fast as possible. But, more important, they prefer to work as our suppliers or employees rather than as our allies. In case of Russian occupation they would like to be able to point out that they have just done a "job" without active political support of the West. There is hardly a day when Allied Intelligence agencies do not find out that war material is being shipped from the Ruhr to the East, and at the Moscow Trade Conference in April 1952, German industry was represented by an impressive delegation, led by Ludwig Krumm, West Germany's No. 1 leather manufacturer who returned with an order for shoes amounting to eighteen million marks. This does not mean that the leaders of German industry and the masters of the Ruhr are pro-Communist or pro-Russian. It does mean, however, that they are perfectly aware of the Russian menace and that they prefer to maintain the greatest possible neutrality. To serve us as blacksmiths is good business, involving a minimum of risk. To furnish us in the name of Western solidarity does not mean more dollars but only increases the chances to be taken."*[324] Hence, the West German industrialists married a desire to maximize profits with an insurance policy of protection from the execution squads of the Stasi and MGB in the event of a Soviet/East German invasion of West Germany.

The lobbying efforts of West German businesses and a trade-friendly Adenauer government paid off for the Soviets. West German trade with the USSR totaled $4.2 million in 1952 and rose to $62.6 million in 1955.[325] By 1948 the Soviets revealed itself as a holder of vast amounts of German scrap metal. The Soviets offered 150,000 to 400,000 tons of scrap to Canada and 50,000 tons were shipped to Belgium.[326] In 1952, eighty seven West German firms were placed on a American economic blacklist with the Soviets and the bloc countries. Soviet agents forged contacts with West German firms. They promised select West German firms financial advantages. Furthermore, these Soviet agents promised West German big business that Moscow would *"go easy"* on the West German businessmen after the *"inevitable"* Soviet domination of all of Germany. The Soviets also dispatched agents to West Germany to set up new firms and even factories, whose workers would be well paid and whose owners were on good terms with the trade unions. These agents would be very well financed.[327]

British trading firms used West German (amongst others) ports to export capitalist goods with the USSR. These exports averaged 10,000-20,000 tons a month. One Ruhr industrialist noted: *"The only persons deluded appear to be the American taxpayers, who presumably believe that effective controls are being exercised."*[328]

---

[323] Berghahn, Volker. Quest for Economic Empire: European Strategies of German Big Business in the Twentieth Century (Berghahn Books, 1996) pages 126-135.
[324] Habe, Hans. Our Love Affair with Germany (Putnam, 1953) page 148.
[325] Stent, Angela. From Embargo to Ostpolitik (Cambridge University Press, 2003) page 29.
[326] Mullaney, Thomas E. "Trade Here Eager for German Scrap" New York Times June 13, 1948 page F1.
[327] Raymond, Jack. "87 German Groups on US Blacklist" New York Times June 4, 1952 page 8.
[328] "Soviet Gets Prohibited Goods" New York Times June 5, 1950 page 2.

West Germany under the CDU-CSU governments of Chancellor Adenauer continued to accept and even pursue trade relations with the USSR. From 1952 to 1955, West Germany became the Soviets' third most important Western European trade partner. The very substantial Soviet orders to West German shipyards (DM 100 million by December 1953, DM 500 million by March 1954) were encouraged by the export policy of the Economics Ministry. The first West German attempts to arrange a general trade agreement with the Soviets came via the West German private sector and were supported by the United States. In response to a Soviet inquiry, members of the West German steel industry met with Soviet foreign trade officials in Copenhagen in August 1952. Economics Minister Erhard favored renewed contacts with the Soviets, but refused to let the meeting take place until he had *"informed the Allies and obtained their permission."* Detailed suggestions for the use of West German economic and financial strength to bring forth Soviet political concessions came from Economics Minister Erhard. He was convinced that *"economic concessions ... carry substantial weight"* in Soviet calculations and he understood that *"our present state of economic development puts us in the position to offer significant economic compensation for important political concessions."* Erhard suggested that Adenauer could offer *"generous export credits, perhaps even in the form of transferable DM."* On September 10, Foreign Minister Hallstein waved some economic bait in a short speech devoted to the advantages to be derived from a *"revival of the traditional trade between the Federal Republic and the Soviet Union"* and the need for discussions about the volume and composition of an exchange of goods.[329] In 1958, Krupp did business with the Soviet bloc totaling $10 million with the USSR being the biggest customer. Mikoyan told Krupp executive Berthold Beitz that *"provided we have the benefit of technological advice from the West. Krupp wares have a great name in Russia. And a canny businessman always keeps two irons in the fire."* Khrushchev noted to Beitz that *"the Soviet Union has entertained good trade relations with the Krupp firm in Essen in the past."* Alfried Krupp announced that his firm had completed contracts for *"substantial sales of railroad and construction equipment,"* and that negotiations for a new treaty with the Soviet Union had begun. Krupp noted that Soviet satellite countries received 6% of Krupp's business. Krupp also elaborated further, when he stated that *"We are of the opinion that this should be increased."*[330] One historian noted that *"Since the war, the Krupp empire, which provided the hardware for Hitler's battle against Communist Russia, turned tail and climbed into bed with the Soviets through a series of cozy business deals. Shifting to the production of steel and other industrial paraphernalia, rather than guns, it opened a vast new market in Russia, offering the commissars rock-bottom prices and highly generous credit terms."* In 1957, Krupp supplied the Soviet Union with a chemical plant and a synthetic fiber complex at a discounted price. In 1958, Beitz, visited the Soviet Union and publicly displayed a chumminess with Soviet officials. This provoked a sharp rebuke from Chancellor Adenauer, who accused Beitz of pursuing a policy that was *"sabotaging"* West Germany's national interests. Beitz sharply replied that *"What could be more logical than to shake hands with a customer who buys*

---

[329] Spaulding, Robert Mark. <u>Osthandel and Ostpolitik: German Foreign Trade Policies in Eastern Europe from Bismarck to Adenauer</u> (Berghahn Books, 1997) pages 373-375

[330] Manchester, William. <u>The Arms of Krupp</u> (Bantam Books, 1973) Accessed From: http://libertyparkusafd.org/lp/Hancock/CD-ROMS/GlobalFederation%5CWorld%20Trade%20Federation%20-%2091%20-%20The%20Arms%20of%20Krupp.html

$1-2-5 million worth of goods from you?"[331] Khrushchev toasted Krupp in the presence of Carl Hundhausen, the Krupp agent in charge of the exhibit, with the following strange-sounding assertion: *"Tell Herr Krupp that he is the kind of capitalist we Communists can do business with…We intend a long association with him."*[332]

By the end of the late 1960s, Soviet documents clearly pointed out the successes the USSR had in lobbying business circles in lobbying for increased trade. In September 1969, KGB Chairman Yuri Andropov reported that a confidant of SPD official Egon Bahr observed *"…there are forces within West German industrial circles who are prepared to assist the normalization of relations with the USSR, but their opportunities are limited in that the economic ties between West Germany and the USSR are still 'embryonic.'"* Andropov also noted that *"…the leadership of another party in power in West Germany - the CDU - is also taking steps to establish unofficial contacts with Soviet representatives and has expressed a willingness to conduct 'a broad dialogue to clarify many issues' for both sides."*[333]

A number of West German companies exported dual use technologies and weapons to the military-industrial complexes of the USSR and East Germany. It was reported in Der Spiegel that *"Despite the Cold War and class struggle…bizarre deals between Western capitalists and Eastern socialists were not unusual. As new Stasi documents show, IMES*[334] *managers established a dense network of Western mediators and dealers for arms trades at the order of the state-absolutely secret also in their own country."*[335]

Former Soviet Defense Ministry official and lawyer Avraham Shifrin noted that *"In 1971 I heard the same complaints from friends still working in the military industry particularly in R&D bureaus and laboratories for lasers and nuclear energy. My friends told me that without imported equipment especially from the United States and West Germany they simply could not work."* Shifrin noted that weapons laboratories were equipped with machinery and tools from West Germany (amongst many other capitalist countries). Shifrin concluded that *"It is only with trade and financial help from the United States that the USSR can produce modern attack weapons against your own country, the United States of America."*[336] West German industrialist Werner J. Bruchhausen formed a network of about 20 electronics front companies that were controlled from West Germany. Bruchhausen and his network diverted more than $10 million in American-made semi-conductor mass production technology from California to Western Europe to the Soviet Union between 1977 and 1980.[337] West German firms shipped 3,000 advanced machine tools from 1985 to 1989 to the Soviet Union. A 26-axis composite tape-laying machine

---

[331] Ibid.

[332] "Krupp Finds Red Trade Boobytrap" Galveston News October 8, 1959 page 8.

[333] Bukovsky, Vladimir. "Book Excerpt: Judgment in Moscow" Breitbart November 27, 2013 Accessed From: http://www.breitbart.com/Big-Peace/2013/11/27/Judgement-in-Moscow

[334] IMES was an East German trading company that was involved in many economic activities, including weapons proliferation.

[335] "GDR Cooperation with Western Arms Dealers Noted" Der Spiegel June 22, 1992

[336] US House of Representatives, Committee on Banking and Currency, Subcommittee on International Trade "International Economic Policy" (GPO Washington DC 1974) pages 279-281.

[337] Gulick, Thomas. "Technology Transfer: Building a Better Beast" World & I February 1987 page 114

sold by Waldrich Siegen was installed directly into an aircraft factory in the USSR. In 1991, that machine churned out entire composite wing structures for the Soviet MiG-29 jet fighter.[338] East Germany also proposed to work with electronics firms in Japan (Toshiba), South Korea (Samsung), Taiwan, and Red China. Toshiba worked with East Germany and KoKo for a long time in acquiring embargoed computers. In 1986, Toshiba agreed to cooperate with East Germany in the construction of a computer chip production facility.[339] These computers provided a boost for the East German computer industry, which produced products that were incorporated into Soviet military weapons systems. In April 1970, the West German firm Salzgitter pledged to build a electro-steel plant in Henningsdorf near East Berlin. The plant cost 70 million DM and Demag and AEG Telefunken participated in the construction of the steel mill.[340] The steel industry is crucial for the development of an arms industry of any consequence in a developed nation.

A high level West German official noted *"While our trade may help the USSR, it helps the German economy even more."*[341] Horst Empke of the West German Social Democratic Party (SPD) noted in 1988 to Business Week journalist Sol Sanders that *"Yes, you can say there is an alliance between some of the enterprise heads in the private sector and our party's policy on aid to the Soviets. They would like to see government subsidies as a way to renovate and convert to other product lines. We would like to see them to help Gorbachev and perestroika."* F. Wilhelm Christians of Deutsche Bank noted *"We have lost our markets in Latin America. We must and can develop new markets in the Soviet Union."*[342]

There was also some evidence which pointed to the successful, strategic Soviet economic penetration of the West German economy. In 1971, the Ost-West Handelsbank AG was established in West Germany. At the end of 1974, the assets of the Ost-West Handelsbank AG totaled $559 million. One West German bank complained that the Ost-West Handelsbank greatly diverted the financing for Soviet imports from other private West German banks.[343] Soviet-made titanium was used by Italy and West Germany in their Tornado fighters.[344] This placed a key aspect of the West German defense industry at the mercy of the Soviet Union. In wartime, these exports would assuredly be terminated, which would force Bonn to shop elsewhere for titanium. West German investments in the USSR also assisted the modernization of the special hard currency Beriozka shop system. In September 1989 the Spar concern of West Germany opened a

---

[338] "COCOM decontrols all" Mednews May 27, 1991

[339] Macrakis, Kristie. Seduced by Secrets (Cambridge University Press 2008) Accessed From: http://worldtracker.org/media/library/Intelligence%20&%20Espionage/Seduced%20by%20Secrets%20Inside%20the%20Stasi's%20Spy-Tech%20World.pdf

[340] Rutherford, Malcolm. "Salzgitter to Build Plant in East Germany" Financial Times April 30, 1970 page 30.

[341] Jamgotch, Nish. Sectors of Mutual Benefit in US-Soviet Relations (Duke University Press, 1985) pages 30-31.

[342] Sanders, Sol. Living Off the West (Madison Books, 1990) pages 157-159.

[343] Central Intelligence Agency. "Soviet and East European Owned Banks in the West" December 1975 Accessed From: http://www.foia.cia.gov/sites/default/files/document_conversions/89801/DOC_0000233296.pdf

344 McForan, Desmond. The World Held Hostage (Oak-Tree Books, 1986) pages 215-216.

Western style joint venture supermarket in Moscow. It was hidden inside the Peking hotel near the US Embassy. Customers can only pay in Deutschmarks.[345]

West Germany loaned $2.1 billion in May 1988 to the USSR to buy West German machinery. Defense Secretary Frank Carlucci noted that *"We are unhappy about these kinds of loans. It puts an extra burden on our defense forces."*[346] The single largest Western loan to the Soviet Union was by a consortium of West German banks; granted in October 1988, it is $1.7 billion line of credit.[347] In June 1989, the Soviet Union signed a contract to buy 300,000 computers worth $750 million for its schools from the West German firm Siemens AG, a giant West German electronics company. Elements within the Defense Department objected, but they were overruled by Secretary of Commerce Mosbacher and Secretary of Defense Cheney.[348]

West German intelligence and Kohl's CDU/CSU government were well-informed of secret trade deals between West German companies and the East Germany mega-trade company Commercial Coordination (KoKo). These deals included the provisioning of West German-made weapons to East Germany.[349] The following West German companies violated the COCOM controls on high technology exports that had a dual-use purpose: Siemens, Hoescht, Horn & Gorwitz, Diebold Deutschland, Leybold-Heraus, Mannesmann, and Rohde & Schwarz. For example, Rohde & Schwarz exported items such as electronic encryption and wireless technology to East Germany.[350]

A CIA report from 1986 titled <u>West Germany as a Target of the East Bloc for the Acquisition of High Technology</u> harshly criticized West Germany for allowing and even encouraging the flow of high technology from West Germany to the USSR and East Germany. Chancellor Helmut Kohl and the CDU-CSU government were also accused of leading the pack in turning a blind eye to this trade. Leybold-Heraus was one of East Germany's closest West German capitalist partners, which made annual profits in the 1980s of over than one billion DM. Throughout most of the 1980s, East Germany purchased 96 million DM worth of equipment such as crystal making machinery, cathode equipment, and plasma etchers from Leybold. Leybold also conducted trade with the Soviet Union, some of which was legal and some illegal. Leybold was concerned that West German customs authorities would detect the trade with East Germany and USSR in the face of increased American pressured under President Reagan. The Stasi sent Siegfried Schurer from the trade division to assist Leybold in smuggling this

---

[345] Cornwell, Rupert. :Out of the USSR: Guilt spoils the joy of Moscow's new cornucopia" <u>The Independent</u> September 29 1989

[346] Shelton, Judy. <u>The Coming Soviet Crash</u> (Free Press, 1990) page 120.

[347] Aron, Leon. "Orchestrating Retreat: Moscow in the Changing Europe of the 1990s" <u>Heritage Foundation Reports</u> January 1, 1990

[348] Auerbach, Stuart. "U.S. Relaxes Computer Sales Curbs" <u>Washington Post</u> July 19, 1989 page A1.

[349] "Reports Say W. German Government Well Informed on Shady E. German Deals" <u>Associated Press Worldstream</u> May 31, 1994

[350] "COCOM List" DDR Lexikon Accessed From: http://translate.google.com/translate?hl=en&sl=de&u=http://www.ddr-wissen.de/wiki/ddr.pl%3FCoCom-Liste&prev=/search%3Fq%3DMauer%2Band%2BDDR%2Band%2B%2522BRD%2Bfirmen%2522%26hl%3Den%26tbo%3Dd%26biw%3D1441%26bih%3D608&sa=X&ei=56PfUPHcF5Dq8gSXwIHAAg&ved=0CFAQ7gEwAw

technology to the USSR and East Germany. Macrakis observed that *"Leybold's greed was limitless."*[351]

In 1988, the West German firm Siemens AG supplied the East Germans with radiation detection equipment.[352] East Germany purchased three Airbus A-310-330 airliners for the state-owned airline Interflug in 1988 with the assistance of Franz Josef Strauss.[353] The radiation detection equipment could have been potentially used by East German troops during occupational and decontamination duties in the West in the immediate aftermath of a conventional-nuclear war with NATO. The Airbus airliners could have also been used to transport Stasi/HVA agents to the Free World for espionage and sabotage duties. The Airbus planes could have been utilized by the East German air force to ferry troops for an invasion of West Germany and/or to dispatch troops for occupation duties.

The Swiss electronics manufacturer MEBO AG transformed Swiss Telekom and Motorola pagers into detonators. The Stasi ordered 40 of these devices in 1988 and they were then passed to Libya.[354] East Germany utilized British companies to ship Heckler and Koch submachine guns destined for the Stasi's special operations units.[355] KoKo allegedly purchased 1,993 Western made weapons and 246 night vision devices from capitalist countries during the period 1980-1989.[356] Siemens sold model S-4000 computers the Stasi. They were maintained by Siemens technicians who travelled to East Germany until 1985.[357]

The production of ammunition in a factory in Spreewald for the East German National People's Army and the Border Troops were produced by machine tools and lathes manufactured by Eastern Bloc countries and West Germany. Ammunition was also produced from machines imported from the West German arms company Fritz Werner Industrial Equipments Co., Ltd. Parts of the barbed wire fence that comprised the Inner-German border was supplied by a West German firm. The ammunition for the SM-70 automatic firing guns on the Inter-German border was produced in East German plants by West German-made precision machinery.[358]

---

[351] Macrakis, Kristie. Seduced by Secrets (Cambridge University Press 2008) Accessed From: http://worldtracker.org/media/library/Intelligence%20&%20Espionage/Seduced%20by%20Secrets%20Inside%20the%20Stasi's%20Spy-Tech%20World.pdf

[352] "Western Germany Siemens to supply equipment to monitor radioactivity" West German Press Agency April 21, 1988

[353] "EEC contract for purchase of A-310 Airbus airliner" East German News Agency July 7, 1988

[354] Deutsch, Anthony. "Swiss company supplied East German secret police with bomb makings" Associated Press June 19, 2000

[355] Leppard, David. "British Companies Funded Stasi" The Sunday Times November 27, 1994

[356] Costelloe, Kevin. "International News" Associated Press Worldstream March 24, 1994

[357] "German News Magazine Focus: Siemens Maintained Stasi Computer" Accessed From: http://www.cvni.net/radio/e2k/e2k025/e2k25de.html

[358] "Niklas, Hölle und Kalle" Der Spiegel September 30, 1991 Accessed From: http://translate.google.com/translate?hl=en&sl=de&u=http://www.spiegel.de/spiegel/print/d-13492530.html&prev=/search%3Fq%3D%2522Kommerzielle%2BKoordinierung%2522%2Band%2B%2522westdeutsche%2BFirmen%2522%2Band%2Bmauer%26hl%3Den%26tbo%3Dd%26noj%3D1%26biw%3D1280%26bih%3D822&sa=X&ei=wGjfUNXlLY3i8gSk8oDQAw&ved=0CE0Q7gEwAw and Rottman, Gordon L. The Berlin Wall (Osprey Publishing 2012) page 25.

Military items such as West German sniper rifles, machine guns, target projectors, grenades and special ammunition, and H&K firearms were imported by the East Germans. West German firms such as Rheinmetall and Fritz Werner and the Dutch firm Phillips were involved in this arms trade with East Germany.[359]

The East German SED/Stasi front company Commercial Coordination (KoKo) was alleged to have been utilized by the West German Messerschmidt-Boelkow-Blohm company to ship weapons to Iraq.[360] Arms companies from Austria, Finland, Spain, Sweden, Switzerland and West Germany utilized East German companies to ship weapons to Islamic Iran and Baathist Socialist Iraq.[361]

Starting in the 1950s, departments of the West German government and private corporations started to slowly outsource aspects of their procurement and production of goods to East German factories, where the labor was cheap and controlled. Goods could then be imported into West Germany tariff-free, as mentioned earlier in this chapter. This aspect of the East German trade with the West was similar to the outsourcing of production to Red China and Vietnam, along with the Mexican maquiladoras. In 1956, the West German army bought mosquito netting for its forces from an East German firm. Leon Davico of Politika noted that *"Although the East German press with good reason is against any manifestation of West German militarism and especially against the creation of West German armed forces an East German firm participated in a competition for delivery of special mosquito netting for the West German Bundeswehr! The full irony of the situation can be understood only if you know that no East German firm can submit tenders in foreign countries-even West Germany-without the permission of the foreign trade authorities of the Pankow government. The absurdity of the situation became even greater after the West German Bundeswehr, after studying all offers, decided to entrust the East German firm with the manufacture of this military equipment."*[362]

The free traders within the West German political class sought to deepen the economic interdependence between the two Germanys. West German trade official Kurt Leopold noted that *"We have failed to take many steps for fear of helping Pankow or Moscow…When we see the East German officials as Communists, and not as Germans, are we not forcing them to be that way?"* Leopold even admitted that freer trade between East and West Germany would result

---

[359] "Small Contribution" Der Spiegel 40/1992 http://translate.google.com/translate?hl=en&sl=de&u=http://www.spiegel.de/thema/alexander_schalck_golodkowski/dossierarchiv-3.html&prev=/search%3Fq%3D%2522Kommerzielle%2BKoordinierung%2522%2Band%2BBRD%2Band%2Bmauer%2Band%2Bspiegel%26hl%3Den%26tbo%3Dd%26biw%3D1024%26bih%3D571&sa=X&ei=BVXfUIH4C5Sc8wTjxIGwCg&ved=0CFQQ7gEwAw

[360] "MBB Denies Link with Former East German Communist Company" AFX News March 20, 1992

[361] "European States Exported Arms Through Former East Germany" United Press International January 15, 1992

[362] Radio Free Europe Research GDR East German Firm Producing Equipment for West German Army December 18, 1956 Accessed From: http://www.osaarchivum.org/greenfield/repository/osa:fdf76c00-e21e-4f99-b016-f7d01c6bf8ff

in the dislocation of West German glassware, optics, and precision machinery industries. Leopold presumptuously noted that *"the West Germans are willing to make these sacrifices."*[363]

Even East German-made goods were sold for hard currency. Kurt Schmeisser, Director General of the Leipzig Fair stated that *"There are some things that we have developed that cannot be made available for the home market."* The chief editor of the East German publication German Foreign Policy Hans W. Aust noted that printing of Western publications was a major source of hard currency for East Germany. Joachim Kranz of the state-owned Book Import and Export Company remarked that Western publishers could get their books and publications manufactured for 50% less than the cost of printing in the West. Kranz noted *"There is a difference in the two economic systems. Labor and paper costs are going up in the West. Here we have stable fixed prices (and wages). In the Western countries they want to make profits. Here we try to meet requirements therefore the prices aren't so high."*[364]

By the late 1970s, an increased number of West German and even other European companies inked contracts for the production of various components in East German factories. Starting in 1976, larger numbers of Western companies desired to use cheap East German labor for production. These goods were produced by East German state-owned companies and then exported back to the West. Some of these Western products produced in East German firms found their way to the Intershops, the Delikat, and Exquisit retail chains. Some products manufactured by East German firms that were subcontracted by West German companies included Salamander brand shoes (from Weissenfels and Meissen), Trumpf chocolates and cocoa powder, Bosch radios (Blaupunkt car radios), BAT cigarettes, Varta batteries, Triumph lingerie, Schiesser underwear, and Beiersdorf (Nivea). The total number of Western products produced in East Germany totaled 120. Four cylinder engines and modern transmissions were produced in East Germany for Volkswagen.[365] In 1978, France agreed to build a Citroen transmissions plant in East Germany. The East Germans re-exported the finished products to France.[366] In February 1984, Volkswagen inked an agreement with East Germany for that communist country to produce 100,000 engines for re-export to West Germany.[367]

It was reported in 1983 that various West German industrial firms outsourced production to East Germany for their lower labor and production costs. The firms/products in question included Tengelmann (cigarettes), shoes (Salamandar), clothing, chocolates, furniture, and even Bundeswehr army uniforms. Textile workers unions estimated that this outsourcing of production to East Germany resulted in job losses totaling 2,500 in 1982.[368] By 1989, some 20 West German firms manufactured products in East Germany. These Western firms that utilized East German labor included Adidas (sportswear), Beiersdorf (cosmetics), Salamander (shoes), and Volkswagen (cars).[369]

---

[363] Dulles, Eleanor Lansing. Berlin The Wall Is Not Forever (University of North Carolina Press, 1967) pages 113-116.
[364] Boner, J. Russell. "Communists & Currency" Wall Street Journal April 18, 1966 page 12.
[365] "Gestattungsproduktion" DDR Lexikon Accessed From: http://www.ddr-wissen.de/wiki/ddr.pl?Gestattungsproduktion
[366] "East Germany gets Citroen unit" Globe and Mail June 8, 1978
[367] "Volkswagen to sign deal with East Germany" United Press International February 9, 1984
[368] Coutu, Diane L. "Inter-German Trade Deals Criticized" Wall Street Journal April 18, 1983 page 31.
[369] Business Europe Volumes 29-30 1989 page 226

The East Germans also created 100 joint ventures with West German businesses. The East German authorities noted: *"the GDR simply will not act as an extended workbench for the FRG; nor will it participate in unprofitable projects. Joint ventures must also be based on the principle of reciprocity."* Western firms such as Nivea, Blaupunkt, and Adidas erected factories in East Germany and they received payment in kind, with the rest of the products allocated to Intershops, Delikat, and Exquisit retail chains. These shops catered to foreigners and wealthy East Germans. SED official Gunter Mittag noted joint ventures acquired the *"technical knowhow from abroad which could not be appropriated in any other way."*[370] Ideas were floated around by East German officials, Bavarian businessmen, and West German political leaders for the creation of *"special economic zones"* in the Saxony and Thuringia regions in East Germany.[371] In other words, the East Germans followed the Soviet and Red Chinese examples in ensuring that the joint venture enterprises and outsourcing assisted the East German state with valuable technologies and goods. Hence, this economic interdependence was to serve the interests of enhancing the power of the SED.

Other Soviet bloc countries in Europe also served as outsourcing hubs for West German companies. In June 1989, Richard Bassett noted that *"For the managers of Krupp, Siemens, Mercedes-Benz and other West German firms who toured Poland earlier this year, Eastern Europe offers cheap labor and the solution to that eternal cry of the German businessman down the decades, new markets."*[372]

Even cheap labor was exported to West Germany from the East. As of June 1986, the West German Building Workers' Union, IG Bau, fought attempts by the Frankfurt city government to use cheap labor from East Germany and other Soviet bloc countries for construction projects. The union reported that 2,000 East Germans and possibly another 2,000 men from Hungary, Romania, and Poland, labored at *"cut rates"* on construction projects in West Germany. Many work long hours and were housed apart from West Germans. A union official noted that East European laborers in West German were working at *"dumping prices"* of DM 10 to DM 15 ($4 to $6) an hour less than West German construction workers. The union official stated that these laborers lived *"in sealed-off barracks during the week, they have hardly any contact with other people and they go home to East Germany by bus at the weekend."* The union official noted that Soviet bloc governments organized laborers for projects in West Germany in order to obtain hard currency.[373]

Even worse was the East German practice of utilizing prison slaves for the production of goods for export to the West. East German prison slaves manufactured goods for Western corporations such as Aldi, Volkswagen, and the British furniture firm MFI. This business was conducted in the 1970s and 1980s. One East German factory forced prisoners to donate blood, which was then sold to the Bavarian Red Cross. Aldi and Volkswagen imported lamps, tights, and screws from East German prison factories. Britain imported furniture worth 18 million pounds in 1980 from East Germany. In 1982, East Germany exported 2 million pounds worth of toys to Great Britain. A German report noted that Western firms *"profited from prison labor in*

---

[370] Dale, Gareth. Between State Capitalism and Globalization (Peter Lang, 2004) page 219.
[371] Ibid, page 242.
[372] Bassett, Richard. "A Sense of Desperation Grips Herr Honecker's Stalinist Bastion; Gorbachov's Visit to West Germany" The Times (London) June 13 1989
[373] Davies, John. "Builders union calls for ban on 'cheap' E European labour" Financial Times January 14, 1986 page 3.

East Germany." One East German table factory, VEB Tischfabrik Finsterwalde, used prisoners to produce furniture for export. This prison factory exported 80% of its goods to British companies, such as Philip Lait Furniture Limited and MFI. Hans-Georg Golz, a historian specializing in East German-British relations commented that *"Cold war propaganda was one thing, trade was another. For British companies, pragmatism often beat ideology."* The author of a German report on East German prison labor and multinational companies, Tobias Wunschik, noted that *"Western countries had deliberately exploited the low-wage economy of East Germany and could have done more to find out about conditions at the factories…These companies made good business, but preferred to look the other way when it came to the rights of workers…These prisoners not only had to do the more unpleasant, tougher jobs than other workers. They also had to meet higher targets."* Roland Braukmann, a former prison slave in an export-oriented East German factory, reported that spotted cameras made in the same plant in West German shops. He noted *"I had always wondered why no one had cared about us in the West. Now I know why."*[374]

Former East German prisoner Tatjyana Sterneberg reported that she was a prison slave forced to manufacture bedclothes for Western corporations for two years while interned in the Hoheneck women's prison in the mid-1970s. She noted that *"It was terrible…In 1974 there were more than 1,600 women in a prison designed for 650 prisoners. My cell was 30 square metres – and had 24 sleeping places. There were three taps and just one toilet."* She commented further that *"I think it is outrageous that these western companies enriched themselves on the backs of political prisoners in East Germany. That is a scandal."* Other East German prison slaves made goods for the Swedish firm Ikea. Former prison slave Dieter Ott commented that *"Had I known that the cupboard door hinges, door handles and chair casters we were making were destined for Ikea, I would probably have thought it was wonderful. I absolutely wanted to go to the west – working for a western company would have excited me. But no one told us."* Ott made goods for Mewa, an East German state-owned firm that sent those slave labor goods to Ikea. Ott noted that *"The bus which took us to the Ikea work had bars on the windows. We drove through a big metal gate and as soon as we were in the building, there was only neon light. No window, no sunshine."*[375]

Deutsche Welle noted that use of East German prison labor was *"a common practice from which many West German companies also benefited."* Steffen Alisch of Forschungsverbund SED-Staat observed that *"Prisoners were made to do the hardest and dirtiest work, the work that nobody else wanted to do, under the worst conditions."* Reportedly, East Germany hosted 65 production sites for Ikea to produce their good using prison labor. About 1% out of 20,000 East German political prisoners was used for industrial production. Hildigund Neubert, who was in charge of Stasi files in the state of Thuringia, noted that the East German regime *"didn't want to do without it (prison labor)…When amnesties were granted on the GDR's national day, there were complaints from the ministries. They were afraid that without these workers, the economic plan could not be fulfilled."* Deutsche Welle reported that

---

[374] Oltermann, Philip. "UK profited from East German forced labour, Stasi archives report claims" The Guardian January 15, 2014 Accessed From: http://www.theguardian.com/world/2014/jan/15/uk-profited-east-german-forced-labour-stasi-report

[375] "East German prison labour claims spread" The Local May 4, 2012 Accessed From: http://www.thelocal.de/money/20120504-42353.html

"Western companies benefited from the low wages in the GDR, while the West German government had a political interest in trade relations in pursuit of its policy of 'change through rapprochement.'"

Reportedly, 6,000 West German companies conducted business with East Germany. West German businesses which engaged in commercial relations with East German firms included the catalog merchants Quelle and Neckermann, the shoe maker Salamander, the cosmetics firm Beiersdorf, the battery maker Varta, and the spirits maker Underberg. In the 1970s, the East Germans dumped a large warehouse stock of sleeveless aprons and delivered ten million of them to West Germany. Quelle purchased these aprons for a few pennies each, put them together into packs of three and offered them for 9.99 marks in its catalog. Quelle generated 30 million DM in profits. East Germany delivered a massive number of foods to the West, such as whole sides of pork, fruit and vegetables. West Berlin was almost dependent on fresh food supplies from East Germany. Deutsche Welle also noted that *"Basic materials, machinery and plans were delivered to the GDR. Finished or processed goods came back. A portion of the production remained in the country, adding to the goods on offer in Intershop hard-currency stores."*[376] Even Dutch firms utilized the slave labor of imprisoned East Germans. These firms included Wehkamp (retail chain), Phillips (technology), Shell (oil), Hema (retail chain), and C&A (retail chain). The prisoners earned little to no money for their hard labor. Often, these prisoners were East German dissidents, political prisoners, and individuals caught trying to escape across the Inter-German border.[377]

Declassified archives revealed that the CDU/CSU government of Chancellor Kohl intended to promote the outsourcing of production to East Germany. In September 1987, Honecker briefed the Politburo of the SED on his visit to West Germany and noted that the political climate towards East Berlin was positive. The enthusiasm of West German big business for outsourcing production to East Germany were very apparent in this report to the SED's Politburo. The document reported: *"The first official visit of Comrade Erich Honecker to the FRG was a significant political success for the GDR and an important result of its politics of reason and realism. The visit is the most significant event in GDR-FRG relations since the signing of the Basic Treaty. It is of farreaching impact and historical significance…This delivered a powerful blow to all revanchist and 'intra-German' efforts… It is significant that a CDU/CSU-led government in particular was forced to agree to the visit and the course of events in this form. It could not avoid taking into account the postwar situation in Europe and the will of the majority of the FRG's population for peace, détente, and normal relations with the GDR. The events and results of Comrade Erich Honecker's visit reflect the enhanced prestige of the GDR, the strength of its peace policies, and its increased international influence… Based on the FRG's role in securing peace in Europe, the visit was a significant step in continuing to bind the FRG to the process of peaceful coexistence. The confrontational policies of the United States were counteracted, and, in the process, the FRG continued to highlight differences between its interests and those of the United States. Thus, the GDR made an important contribution to the practical implementation of the peace policies of the socialist states, especially the momentous initiatives of M(ikhail) Gorbachev and the summit conference of the Warsaw Pact in Berlin. The*

---

[376] Birkenstock, Gunther. "East Germany relied on forced labor" Deutsche Welle June 5, 2012 Accessed From: http://www.dw.de/dw/article/0,,15932840,00.html

[377] Marvin Hokstam "Dutch Companies Used Cheap DDR Labor" January 24, 2014 http://www.nl-times.nl/node/16464

*visit carried great international weight. It is a significant contribution toward improving the climate in Europe and continuing to firm up the international position of the GDR. It strengthens the GDR as an equal partner in its relations with capitalist industrial countries…Comrade Erich Honecker's assertive manner contributed decisively to the comprehensive and convincing presentation of the policies of the socialist German state and the (other) socialist states on the issues of peace, disarmament, and détente. He also strengthened the position of the realistic forces within the ruling circles of the FRG, promoting a coalition of reason and realism, and he reinforced the process of differentiation within the government coalition, extending into the CDU/CSU. The German Communist Party, the peace movement, and all democratic, peace-loving forces in the FRG were supported. The visit positively influenced support for the policies of the SPD… **It was agreed that economic cooperation between combines (Kombinate) and foreign trade companies in the GDR and companies in the FRG should be further developed and that, in doing so, forms of cooperation such as collaborative efforts in the exportation of installations and equipment, particularly to third markets, and in the production of goods by West German companies in the GDR (Gestattungsproduktion)1, should be more strongly developed; The German term 'Gestattungsproduktion' literally refers to the fact that West German companies were 'allowed' (gestattet) to produce goods in the GDR – eds**.*"[378]

There were also occasions where the East German government and Western corporations exploited their greed for hard currency and profits through surreptitious medical experiments and product testing on East German citizens. In 1988, East Germany allowed the West German company Hoechst AG to test its high blood medication on East German citizens. Hoechst was attracted to the common language, culture, well-trained East German medical staff, discretion offered by a dictatorship, and low cost of conducting a study in a soft currency communist country. West Germany considered the drug a danger to human life and paid the East Germans 500,000 DM to conduct the study in that communist country.[379]

Japanese and West German chemical companies reportedly paid the East Germans tested non-approved medicines on their citizens from 1984 to 1989. East Germany earned 17 million deutschmarks in 1989 alone from this program. Participating capitalist companies included Bayer (subsidiary of Hoechst-West Germany), Chemie Linz AG (Austria), and Asahi Chemical (Japan). It was noted that: *"The experiments on human beings, which…West German companies participated in, were one of the dirtiest businesses with which the (communist) regime got hold of the urgently needed hard currency."*[380]

A subsidiary of Degussa, Asta Homburg tested drugs on the East German population with the permission of the communist government. This program was laid out in negotiations between the East Germans and Homburg at the Leipzig Trade Fairs in the late 1960s. Homburg saved money through these experiments, thus increasing their profits.[381]

---

[378] "SED Politburo draft of September 15, 1987, on the official visit by Erich Honecker to the Federal Republic of Germany from September 7-11, 1987" Accessed From: http://ghdi.ghi-dc.org/sub_document.cfm?document_id=1148

[379] Zatlin, Jonathan. The Currency of Socialism (Cambridge University Press 2007) page 188.

[380] "Report: Western firms used East Germans to test medicines" United Press International February 4, 1991

[381] "West German Pharma Company Tested Products on Eastern Athletes" Deutsche Presse-Agentur August 14, 1998

In 1989, the West German company Berliner Import/Export GmbH contracted with the East German government and Western corporations to test pharmaceuticals on East German citizens. East Germany earned $11 million in hard currency by conducting these tests. The East German firm Berliner Import/Export GmbH took a 30% cut of the profits. Those who ingested the drugs experienced symptoms such as mild nausea and fevers to hair loss, heart palpitations, and tremors.[382]

Russia's ambitions for an alliance with Germany continue unabated, despite the fall of the Berlin Wall and half of Germany no longer being communist. No longer is a communist or Russian invasion a necessity for Moscow to gain control over Germany. Instead, Germany's political and economic elites and former Stasi agents and SED officials served as handmaidens for Russian power in the Federal Republic. What Moscow failed to achieve by traditional military force, it attained through economic warfare and influence operations directed to the German political class.

The last item that should be explored is *"What should the US policy be in respects to the emerging Russo-German alliance?"* The following policies should be explored by the United States government under control by Democrats and Republicans who represent the interests of American nationalism and not globalism or progressive leftism. Such policy proposals would include:

1) Assert continued American friendship with Germany and support for anti-Russian elements within the CDU/CSU of the Federal Republic.
2) Stepped up covert monitoring of possible BND-SVR cooperation against American interests.
3) As a means of containing possible predatory Russian and German trade practices, the United States should withdraw from the Trans-Atlantic Partnership (TTIP) trade talks. Since Russia has a tremendous economic presence in Germany, Moscow could use the *"openness"* and further *"liberalization"* of trade with Western Europe to insert front companies and attempt to dump more goods into the American market. Such actions would further destroy the already impaired US productive base. Such trade agreements also would impair American sovereignty in respect to domestic economic policy making.
4) Withdrawal from the sovereignty destroying World Trade Organization, of which Russia and Germany are members. Berlin and Moscow should not have veto power over any sovereign American trade policy decisions that might be made in our national interests in contravention to the interests of the *"global"* economy and multinational companies.
5) Covertly monitor goods and technologies sold by American companies to Germany on the grounds that such items may be transshipped to Russia.
6) Revocation of PNTR for Russia.
7) Stepped up American efforts to develop natural gas and oil reserves within the borders of the United States and negotiate exports of these energy resources to Germany in an effort to wean Berlin's dependence off of Moscow.
8) Retention of American military bases in Germany as a means of signaling to Moscow our resolve in containing Putin's power projections.

---

[382] "Human Experiments" Multinational Monitor March 1991 Accessed From: http://www.multinationalmonitor.org/hyper/issues/1991/03/lines.html

Made in the USA
Charleston, SC
27 January 2017